From Baggy Greens To A Blue Suit

Tony Easterby

www.mbspress.com

Copyright © 2014 Tony Easterby

The moral right of Tony Easterby to be identified as the Author of the work has been asserted by them in accordance with the Copyright, Designs and Patents Act 1988. All rights reserved. No part of this book may be used or reproduced by any means, graphic, electronic, or mechanical, including photocopying, recording, taping or by any information storage retrieval system without the written permission of the publisher except in the case of brief quotations embodied in critical articles and reviews.

National Library of Australia Cataloguing-in-Publication entry

Author: Easterby, Tony, author.
Title: From baggy greens to a blue suit / Tony Easterby.
ISBN: 9781921883637 (paperback)
Subjects: Easterby, Tony.
            Australia. Army. Royal Australian Regiment. Battalion, 4th.
            Australia. Royal Australian Air Force.
            Soldiers--Australia--Biography.
            Police--Australia--Biography.

Dewey Number: 355.0092

Publishers Details

MBS Press

A division of the Pickawoowoo Publishing Group.

Contact Details: info@mbspress.com

Western Australia

Printed & Channel Distribution

Lightning Source | Ingram (USA/UK/AUS)

For personal copies signed by the author please email Tony Easterby [teasterb@bigpond.net.au]

PREFACE

The first section of this book concerning the Author's Army service as an Infantry Soldier with the Royal Australian Regiment was first published in 2002 as a novel called GREEN MULES GREEN GIANTS. It is only fitting therefore that the contents of that book be once again used to complete the overall picture of how the Author left behind an Army career in baggy greens to wear a blue suit of the Royal Australian Air Force.

Very little has been changed concerning the Author's Army career, other than some new photographs. The second section of this book involving the Author's 16 year service with the RAAF, as a RAAF Policeman, is published for the first time.

A lot of facts, possibly a little fiction and I hope a lot of humour.

Tony Wayne Easterby

ACKNOWLEDGEMENTS

A special thanks to those members of the 2nd and 4th Battalions of the Royal Australian Regiment with whom I had the privilege to serve. Also for their stories and friendship.

A special mention of ex Warrant Officer R.R. (Jock) Richardson. MM. MID ex 4 RAR (now deceased) who helped shape those early years of my army life.

My good friend of many years Kevin Rideout (now deceased) who supplied several of the Borneo photos in this book. Kevin was my section commander in Malaysia/Borneo from 1966-1967.

I would also like to thank all those dedicated men and women of the RAAF, The Service Police, RAAF Police and RAAF Police Dog handlers with whom I had the privilege of serving. Thank you.

Last but not least my darling wife Joy for her patience, understanding and help with this book. Without her help this book would not have been possible. Thank you my love.

Contents

1. THE MAKING OF A SOLDIER – 20 APRIL 1964..........9
2. ARRIVAL AND TRAINING – MALAYSIA – 1965 15
3. DOWN MEMORY LANE – MALAYSIA – 1965 TO 1967..25
4. A MEMBER OF WHERE THE F..K ARE WE TRIBE – PART1 28
5. RELAXATION – PARACHUTING – SOUTH AUSTRALIA/MALAYSIA 34
6. BORNEO – APRIL 1966 TO SEPTEMBER 1966..........41
7. RETURN TO TERENDAK GARRISON 64
8. ARRIVAL IN AUSTRALIA AND PREPARATION FOR VIETNAM..................................66
9. HEADING FOR VIETNAM ON BOARD AIRCRAFT CARRIER HMAS SYDNEY (THE VUNG TAU FERRY) – 21MAY1968...67
10. ARRIVAL IN VIETNAM 1968..70
11. NUI DAT (PHUOC TUY PROVINCE) 72
12. THE SECTION – Vietnam 73
13. OPERATIONS VIETNAM 1968 – PIGS CAN FLY.......77
14. NUI DAT – VIETNAM – A FRIDGE FOR THE BOYS 80
15. OPERATIONS VIETNAM – BATTALION ATTACK – 1968 84
16. OPERATIONS VIETNAM – BRAVE SOULS 88

17.	FRIENDLY TROOPS –VIETNAM – 1968	94
18.	A MEMBER OF WHERE THE F..K ARE WE TRIBE – PART 2	97
19.	THE PLASTIC BULLET – VIETNAM – 1968	102
20.	LANDMINE – VIETNAM	105
21.	TYPICAL DAYS IN THE JUNGLE – VIETNAM	107
22.	FINAL PATROL – VIETNAM – 25TH AUGUST 1968	110
23.	THE ENDING OF MY ARMY CAREER	116
24.	TRANSITION – ARMY – RAAF	118
25.	BRIEF HISTORY OF THE ROYAL AUSTRALIAN AIR FORCE POLICE (RAAF SERVICE POLICE)	120
26.	ENLISTMENT AND TRAINING WITH THE RAAF	125
27.	RAAF BASE WILLIAMS, POINT COOK	127
28.	RAAF BASE LAVERTON –VICTORIA	130
29.	N01 STORES DEPOT – RAAF TOTTENHAM	143
30.	RAAF BASE POINT COOK – VICTORIA	151
31.	DETACHMENT B – MELBOURNE	160
32.	RAAF BASE, EDINBURGH, SOUTH AUSTRALIA	162
33.	RAAF BASE BUTTERWORTH – MALAYSIA	165
34.	RECREATION FOR FAMILIES IN MALAYSIA	185
35.	PENANG SHIFT SUPERVISOR	192
36.	LETTERS OF APPRECIATION/THANKS	208
37.	GENERAL PATROLS AROUND PENANG	213

38.	CAR RALLY PENANG	229
39.	TOURS TO THAILAND – THIS SECTION IS DEDICATED TO MY MATE 'BLUE'	232
40.	LEAVING MALAYSIA	252
41.	RAAF BASE – PEARCE – WESTERN AUSTRALIA	256
42.	RAAF BASE – WILLIAMTOWN	264
43.	CONCLUSION	268
44.	ABOUT THE AUTHOR	271
45.	GLOSSARY OF TERMS AND ABBREVIATIONS	272
46.	WEAPONS – GLOSSARY OF TERMS AND ABBREVIATIONS	277

CHAPTER 1

THE MAKING OF A SOLDIER – 20 APRIL 1964

The Author – A1200181 Private Tony Wayne Easterby – Malaysia 1965.

My initial basic training with the Australian Army as a lad of 18 did more good than harm. I found out that there was a lot more to being a soldier than 'Here is a rifle son, we are going to teach you how to kill people with it'. I was given the opportunity to further my education, received adult wages and given the opportunity to travel overseas with good and close friends.

My first destination, after having signed up for the Army in Brisbane, Queensland on the 20th April 1964, was 1RTB Kapooka in Wagga Wagga, New South Wales. Here I was to be trained in basic drill, weapon handling and any other type of training that the Army cared to inflict on me and many others. Kapooka was a hellhole, stinking hot in summer and freezing cold in winter. I had never been away from home before but I was fortunate, as my parents had taught me to wash/iron and to keep my room tidy. Some of the other lads however were not so lucky as they obviously knew nothing about keeping whites separate from colours when they washed their clothes. It was not uncommon to see purple underwear on the line after they had thrown their black beret in with their whites. A lot of new, white underwear had to be purchased, including long johns, before leaving the place after 13 weeks of physical and mental torture.

Our living conditions at Kapooka were pretty rough, we lived in old Nissen Huts, named after Peter Norman Nissen (1871-1930) a British army officer who designed them. They were a prefab building of corrugated iron in the shape of a half cylinder. Our Nissen hut had very few panes of glass left in the windows, the doors were full of holes where they had been used by the previous occupants for bayonet practice and the gaps between the floorboards let the wind and cold whistle through. Most of our hut had the Masonite board lining on the ceiling and walls removed to reveal the bare corrugated iron hut. This made the hut incredibly hot in summer and bloody cold in winter. The

Masonite lining of the hut had no doubt been used by the previous recruits for their bedding inspections. The Masonite was cut up into small square boards and placed in between the folded sheets and blankets which had to be squared off and placed at the head of your bed each morning for inspection purposes. Only one blanket could be used on your single bed each day for inspection and this blanket had to be pulled over the mattress so tight that the inspecting officer could bounce a coin off of it. The bed had to remain in this condition all day until you were ready to go to bed each night. Unfortunately the setting up of the bed for inspection each morning took so long that you could not manage it each and every day. It was not uncommon to see beds/blankets/sheets set up in permanent inspection order for the entire 13 weeks while the soldier slept on the floor alongside the bed, wrapped in his Army Greycoat. In winter this was hell, take it from me, as I was one of those soldiers who slept on the floor beside my bed.

Each soldier had a metal locker beside his bed in the hut and this locker, like the bed, had to be in inspection order at all times. Your hankies, socks, underwear etc. had to be neatly squared off on each shelf so that the inspecting officer could count each and every item. Your uniform shirts, trousers etc. had to be starched/ironed and hung on hangers set at regulated distances within the locker. You were allowed one set of underwear to wear, one set in the wash and the remainder on display in your locker.

The locker, like the bed, took all your time to keep it in inspection order. Everything in the hut had to be dusted each and every day. Home was never like this. It was also not uncommon to spend any of your free time, in the drying rooms watching your underwear and your other clothes dry, so that they did not get stolen. As you were expected to replace, at your own expense, any discoloured underwear or clothes prior to leaving, it was again not uncommon to find your white underwear replaced with a bright purple set. The only good thing about the drying rooms was that they were a great place to sleep during winter.

On looking through my notes involving Kapooka I have circled the word rabbits. One thing that really stood out while I was at Kapooka was the amount of times that we were fed rabbit for meals. Lunch and evening meals, rabbit or rabbit stew it was always the same. Either the government was saving money by feeding us local rabbits, which were all around the place, or someone in the Mess was playing funny buggers with our rations. No bloody wonder I have never eaten another rabbit since I left Kapooka in 1964. Another thing the Army cured me of eating is Brussels sprouts.

We trained day and night at Kapooka and when not training carried out duties such as guard, mess duties and equipment maintenance. I still remember how cold it could get on guard duty at night during the winter months. It did not matter what type of clothing you wore to keep out the cold, you still froze. It was that cold it was painful. A hard 13 weeks believe me, no wonder some of the recruits deserted.

From Kapooka, after being told that I was going to infantry, I was posted to Infantry Training Center, Ingleburn NSW on the 6th August 1964. Here I was to spend another pleasant 13 weeks learning to become an Infantry Soldier. The weather was a little better anyway. While at the center I applied for Special Air Service Regiment training but could not keep up with their strenuous physical training exercises. I am glad in one way that I was not accepted, as the SASR play rough.

Years later while working as a RAAF Policeman, serving at RAAF Base Pearce, Western Australia in 1985, I came across this SASR Sergeant who informed me that he had volunteered for a SASR refresher course in interrogation which was being held on the RAAF Base. The guy had to be a complete nut as he was interrogated over several days, stripped naked in the middle of winter and hosed down in the middle of an open field with a high-pressure fire hose. During the whole time a bag had been placed over his head to prevent him from seeing his interrogators. Who in their right mind would volunteer for something like that? Seeing that I was not cut out to be one of Australia's finest, the Army made me a Rifleman, plain old Private Easterby. I enjoyed Ingleburn; we spent a lot of time on weapon training even if some of the armoury was outdated. The training was thorough as even today after not having handled a SLR (rifle) for over 50 years I still remember how to strip and assemble it blindfold.

My first requested posting as an Infantry Soldier was to the 2nd Royal Australian Regiment, then stationed at Enoggera Army Barracks, Brisbane, Queensland. I joined Delta Company on the 11th November 1964, as a Rifleman. I was born in Brisbane; my family was there, hence my request for a home posting. My first Platoon Commander was a young Lieutenant with the surname of Hudson, naturally we called him 'Rock' (not to his face of course). Lieutenant Hudson was later to join the Special Air Service Regiment and lose his life while on active service in Borneo in 1966 along with another close friend of mine, Private Moncrieff.

I remained with 2RAR until the 27th April 1965, before requesting a transfer to the 4th Royal Australian Regiment then stationed at Woodside, South Australia. The 4th Battalion was going to Malaysia sometime in September 1965.

While stationed with 4RAR at Woodside, prior to leaving Australia, I took up Sports Parachuting with other members of the Regiment. We had formed our own parachute club within the Battalion and jumped out of anything that would get us off the ground. The Four Winds Parachute Club had a big effect on my life. The Battalion also conducted language classes to teach us Malay and Indonesian.

I managed to turn 19 on the 30th August 1965 and moved with 4RAR to Malaysia late September of that year. In May the following year I was in Borneo with the Battalion fighting elements of the Indonesian Army who were making their way into Sabah and Sarawak from the Indonesian State of Kalimantan. Prior to going to Borneo I was hospitalized in Malaysia with Malaria and then Scrub Typhus. I suffered from Malaria attacks throughout my Army Service, part of my RAAF Service and some four years later after leaving the services. My last attack being some 6 years ago.

A Company – 1 Recruit Training Battalion –
(Kapooka Wagga Wagga NSW)
May 1964. The Author, second front row, five in from right hand side.

CHAPTER 2
ARRIVAL AND TRAINING – MALAYSIA – 1965

The Author – age 19. Section Machine Gunner with Bren Gun, Malaysia early 1965. The Bren Gun was converted to fire NATO 7.62 rounds from a 30 round magazine.

I was a 19-year-old serving as a Rifleman in Bravo Company, 4th Royal Australian Regiment. We were in Malaysia and it was 1965. For a very short time I became a number one on the section machine gun, but when the light Bren gun was replaced with a big and heavy British General Purpose Machine Gun (GPMG), tripod mounted, it was time for me to go back to carrying a Rifle.

For me those early years in Malaysia were exciting. I was single, receiving adult wages and having a great time. I had never travelled outside of Australia before and was still very naïve.

Having been flown to Asia from Sydney in 1965, we landed in Singapore. I remember to this day of getting off of the aircraft and walking across the tarmac, the heat of Asia and its unforgettable smell. We left Singapore that night in buses along with the Army families who had travelled with us on the Aircraft. We entered Malaysia via the causeway Johor Bahru.

The buses dropped families off at different married quarters in Malacca a few kilometers from the Commonwealth Garrison. We single men were transported to the base, which was known as Terendak Garrison. Some families who were lucky enough to have been given married quarters within the Garrison remained on the buses with us. The British Garrison (28 Commonwealth Brigade) overlooked Malacca Strait and was the most beautiful Military base I have ever had the privilege to serve on. We were to acclimatize for a week before being allowed out to annoy the local people. I had a mate who had been sent ahead of the Battalion as part of the advance party. My mate, Speedy knew by now how to get out of the Garrison without an identity card, so within a couple of days we were outside of the Garrison eating the local meals while at the same time trying to avoid the Military Police. The reason for the identity cards was that Malaysia still had Communist Insurgents and we were also at war with Indonesia. The Battalion was now using live ammunition and it did not take me long to appreciate that we were no longer playing soldiers, this was the real thing and bullets killed people.

Another important factor that I was to learn very quickly was to be careful where and what I ate outside of the Garrison. I was prepared to try any type of Asian food like shark fin soup and birds nest soup and in doing so picked up a bait. I received a good dose of food poisoning within about five days of my arrival in country. If you have ever suffered from food poisoning, all you want to do is to die and get it over with. So after that, during my two-year tour of Malaysia, I ate nothing but Aussie meals. This was a shame, as 17 years later, I returned to Malaysia with the RAAF only to realize what I had missed out on all those years, that beautiful Asian food.

The Garrison, as I have stated was magnificent, a self-contained City with an Olympic size pool, picture theatre, NAAFI store, Commonwealth club and a beautiful stretch of white sandy beach overlooking Malacca Strait. You had to overlook the barbed wire entanglements around the base and on the beach, all of which were patrolled day and night. We could not have the Communist Insurgents or the Indonesian Army sneaking up on us could we? You could see Indonesia across the other side of the Straight, and it would have been so easy for them to land using small craft even though we had radar. The Garrison had its own airfield, Commonwealth war cemetery and a very modern hospital. We shared the Garrison with several British Military units, including the famous Gurkhas. Two New Zealand Companies were also present; they trained with us and also joined us in Borneo. The Battalions barracks in which we single men lived, were first class, – four guys to a room, – plenty of space and a boot boy outside every block. Our boot boy, who I should say was an elderly gentleman of Indian origin, was named Kim. Kim had worked for the British and Australians for many years and was one hell of a nice guy. Kim would spit polish our boots and shoes using polish on his fingers only, no rags. This use to fascinate me as he would polish boots and shoes from daylight to dawn seven days a week, I would get tired just watching him. Kim would also bring you tea/coffee or a toasted sandwich anytime day or night, he was paid extra of course. After you had been on the booze the night before, Kim was a welcome sight next morning, with that cup of coffee. Kim was also good for a loan if you were short of money before payday, he ran a book where he charged a few dollars interest and no doubt retired a wealthy man.

As a single guy living in on the base I had my clothes washed by the local base laundry. The only problem was that the laundry did not change the washing water after each wash and we all suffered 'Dhobi rash' between the legs and under the armpits. At that time the Army was short of a cure for the rash other than some yellow dye and metho. The cure took more skin off until you bled and you had to seek out local cures. I still bear the scars today left by the rash. The starched jungle greens did not help, as when they were returned from the base laundry you could stand the trousers, shorts and shirts up on the floor by themselves as they were that full of starch. Great for parade, but not much else.

OUT AND ABOUT

Some of the stupid things that I got up to in Malaysia as a single lad leaves me bewildered at times. On one occasion my mate 'Speedy' and I, were out on the town in Malacca and had a few to many beers to drink.(probably two) We decided that we would have a suit made each by one of the town tailors. Trying to outdo each other no doubt we picked the most ridiculous materials. I remember waking up the next morning looking at a silver set of pants and silver coat standing up on the floor by themselves, next to my bed in the hut. For my material I had chosen some form of silver foil, which they now make sunshades out of for motor vehicles. The trousers and jacket not only looked ridiculous but when I got into the suit I could not sit down or bend my arms. I not only felt like Ned Kelly but also looked like the Tin Man from the Wizard of Oz. Kim the boot boy thought the suit was some new bulletproof uniform issued by the Army. I must have looked a sight coming home through the guard gate that night or morning. I could have fought a fire in this suit and not have got burned; it was so thick and heavy. I could not wait to see what my mate, Speedy had chosen. Sure enough his suit was just as bad, pin stripes that wide he looked like Bo-bo the clown in his outfit. Not only were the stripes about three inches wide, they were all colours, it was a suit straight out of a circus. What a sight we must have looked in town. The locals must have thought that they were seeing a quick visit to their country by Elvis and his crew. I remember once we sobered up we could not wait to burn our outfits.

Another time while I was in town trying to escape from the Military Police I got mud all over my white trousers, and to wash the mud off, I jumped into this large wooden dish full of water that was situated on the footpath outside of one of the local shops. I could not understand what all the fuss was about when the locals gathered around complaining about me using the dish to wash in until I had a closer look and saw all their peeled vegetables at the bottom of the dish.

EARLY DAYS IN THE BUSH

On one of our very first patrols into the dark deep jungles of Malaysia we came across what we thought was our very first real Malaysian bushman. It was time to put our language training in Malay to the test. After telling us in perfect Queens English to 'Bugger off, I don't have the faintest idea what the bloody hell you are talking about' we gave up in disgust. I don't believe we used Malay again until we went to Borneo. We think the Dyaks of Borneo understood us, maybe not.

When we were not on sentry duty day or night protecting the Garrison, we were out in the jungle training and also looking for any sign of an enemy. When training, live ammunition was taken from us and replaced with blank training rounds. The only live rounds were carried by the section commanders, a few rounds taped to their dog tags.

It was during one of our training exercises in Malaysia that our best swimmer, Private Robinson drowned while trying to secure a rope so that the rest of the Company could cross a flooded tin mine. He never made it any further than a few meters into the water, with a light rope tied around his waist, before disappearing. Those soldiers close to the bank who saw him disappear dived in to save him but when they got to the light rope he was no longer attached. I don't really know what happened, as we were not informed of the outcome of the investigation. A good soldier and friend who is sadly missed even to this day. The training continued before our deployment to Borneo

The Author age 19 resting outside his Married Quarter in Malacca, Malaysia 1965.

Above – Kim our boot boy, made a fortune as he ran a money lending business between Military Pay days. – 1965-1967.

Below –The Author, on being chosen as Attending Soldier and stood down from Battalion Guard Duty – 1965.

Terendak Garrison Malaysia 1965 – Sections of Bravo Company 4RAR on Parade.

The famous Gurkhas with their legendary Gurkha Khukuri knife cutting the heads off animals in one downward motion. Terendak Garrison Malaysia 1965.

The Gurkha Khukuri knife is one of the oldest blade forms in the history of the world. It has cultural and religious significance. The Gurkhas brought the attention of the knife to the world in India and Nepal. The Gurkhas are probably the best mercenary force the world has ever seen. Author.

CHAPTER 3
DOWN MEMORY LANE – MALAYSIA – 1965 TO 1967

One bloody big Boa Constrictor which took five rounds of 7.62 to kill. This snake was over 6 meters in length.

I don't like snakes; I like them less when they are big enough to eat you. We were again on a training exercise in the deep jungles of Malaysia. A group of us had stopped for a short break; one of our section members was standing apart from us finishing a cigarette. On completion he buried the cigarette stub in the ground and made his way over towards our group. As he left his position, this large snake hit the ground where he had been standing. It was like several car tyres had been dropped from the sky and hit the ground. This was the biggest snake that I have ever seen, and hopefully the last outside of a zoo. The snake, a large boa constrictor, six meters in length with a head twice the size of my hand, dropped down from a tree above in the hope of landing on our mate and crushing him to death before consuming him.

As we were on a training exercise, the only live rounds of ammunition (7.62mm) were held by one of the senior section members. He had five live rounds taped to his dog tags around his neck. As you can imagine, our efforts to rip the five rounds from around his neck, load a rifle magazine and kill the snake, took its toll, on the neck of the trooper that is! I remember the snake, still kicking; being held up by several soldiers on their shoulders while someone took a photograph. A copy of the photograph was to appear in the Australian Pix and Post magazine a few months later.

During another training session in the jungle a few kilometers from the base, we were learning different map reading techniques. Not sure of our exact position on the map, we blundered out of the jungle and onto a logging track. Behold here was our supplier of ice creams, flavoured milk and cold drinks, Smiley, the Magnolia (Milk) man and his little van. I remember asking Smiley as to how he found us, and how did he know we would come out on the logging track. His answer 'You always come out here, after all you are only out the back of the base'. Smart basket!

I remember the first little huts that we came across in the jungles of Malaysia. They were made from sticks and shaped like an Indian tepee; we thought they were made by the enemy to hide in. Imagine our disappointment when we were informed that they were made by the local Malays to hide in while they trapped birds.

On another occasion we were making our way through the jungle on our way back to camp, when a group of us decided to stop and brew up. We were standing around talking, watching our mugs on the boil when from above us in the tree came a growling sound. On looking up we saw we had disturbed a black panther. It was huge and we had woken him with our chatter! I guess I never dreamed that I would come face to face with such a beautiful animal outside of a zoo. After a few seconds to let it sink in that here was this big angry black cat above us, wanting to come down, we departed in all directions. Bugger the mugs and stoves, they could be replaced, it was time for us to see who could reach the base first. I was never much of a distance runner in full pack, but with an incentive like that; I made it to base within the first five troops. I don't know who got the biggest fright the cat or us. I know one thing; I was not going back for a bloody mug and stove! Q-Store here I come.

Our training in Malaysia was to prepare the Battalion for operations in Borneo and later on in Vietnam. I was hoping like hell not to run into any more snakes, panthers, tigers or any other large creatures outside of a zoo. Did I mention tigers, read on.

CHAPTER 4

A MEMBER OF WHERE THE F..K ARE WE TRIBE – PART 1

I always considered myself an average map-reader, especially with an Army map and a compass. You need to be better than average, however, as knowledge of your exact position on a map could mean a matter of life or death.

During my early years of Army service as a 19 year-old, it was easy to waiver responsibility and let someone else be leader. To me it was all just a game; a map and compass got you from A to B and, hopefully back again.

It was on an exercise in Malaysia, a bolt of lightning must have hit me as I accepted the role of Lance Corporal, second in command of a section of 10 men. What made it even worse was that I actually enjoyed the position. Along with the position however came responsibility, and was I ready for such a change in my life? Only time would tell.

I look back now and realize that I must have been fairly accurate with my map reading skills, as each time I arrived no more than a few meters from my objective. More bloody luck than skill.

Only twice did I manage to get lost while in the jungle and both times luck was with me. The first time I did not need a map or a compass as I got lost on a night clearing patrol. Still in Malaysia, we were again on exercise and the Battalion was being assessed on all aspects of infantry training. Each Company and Platoon had an independent inspector with them and we were debriefed at the end of each day as to our good or bad procedures, or general stuff ups! We were also up against an Australian Unit acting as our enemy and who knew all our military tactics. Plastic bullets (blanks) replaced real bullets, and the real bullets were once again sealed up and wrapped around someone's dog tags (metal name tags) around their neck.

As the acting Lance Corporal for my section (6 Platoon B Company) I was told by the section Corporal to carry out a clearing patrol of our perimeter, just on dusk and prior to the Company settling into a harbour position for the night.

We had arrived at our night harbour position, a little late, and it was also a little late to be carrying out a sweep and search of our perimeter. I was to take five men, go out through our own machine gun post, search the jungle to my left for any enemy, and come back in through the next machine gun post. Simple, except it was now pitch black. I had been given a password to use when coming back in through the next machine gun post. I needed more than a bloody password.

By the time we entered the jungle, through our own gun group or machine gun post, I could not see the hand on the end of my arm let alone anything else. Good one Corporal. If we were to find any enemy, we would have had to have fallen over them and they us. I knew I was going to be in trouble five minutes out.

The best I could do was to position one of my patrol members close to the harbour position so that he could remain in contact with other members of the harbour, while the remainder of us spread out over a short distance to carry out the sweep and search to our left.

The bloody jungle was that thick and the night so bloody dark we needed to have held hands to have kept in contact. I was thinking to myself, this is bloody stupid, but then again at my age nothing the Army did made a lot of sense.

Unbeknown to me the harbour section members, who my trooper was to keep in contact with, were sticking to their training and remaining silent as we bashed our way through the jungle. It was only when I thought we had gone far enough that I was to learn that the wacker on the other end of my clearing patrol was not in contact with anyone, as no one in the company would break their silence and talk to him. We could not see each other on the clearing patrol let alone where the rest of the Platoon or Company were.

As luck would have it, we stumbled out of the thick jungle and onto a bush track or logger's track. Without the dense jungle around us we could just make out the dark silhouette of each other. It was decided that we would not yell and scream to try and locate the rest of the Company, as it would not look good on our assessment record. As none of us had a torch, it was decided to make the best of a bad situation and someone suggested a fire.

Some bloody fire. There was not a lot of loose, solid wood close by, at least that we could see, the best we could manage was a few dry leaves. I was not that keen on feeling my way around in the dark looking for firewood as the way my luck was running my piece of wood would turn out to be some bloody big angry cobra snake.

Our roaring fire shone like a single candle and we were lucky to see our boots let alone anything else. Some bright spark (excuse the pun) decided to make a fire torch out of some sticks and leaves, and on doing so decided to look around in the dark for any signs of boot prints other than our own. We knew we had crossed over a track that afternoon just before we followed a creek to the high ground where the Company had decided to harbour for the night. Our bright spark with the fire torch, while looking around on the ground for boot prints made an amazing discovery.

'I can't see many boot prints but there are these big paw prints, looks like tiger tracks!'

'Tiger. Tiger, what bloody tiger?' Came the reply.

We gathered around to look at the so-called Tiger prints.

'If it is not a Tiger it's one bloody big cat' exclaimed another.

'Listen, I'm not staying out here with bloody Tigers running around, I'm for finding Company' said another.

'Me too' replied another.

'Who has the live rounds?' asked another.

'What live rounds? there back with the Corporal, around his neck' explained another

'You mean with the same dumb bum that forgot to tell the rest of the platoon to keep in contact with us on the sweep' asked another.

With a few more fire torchlights, we came across boot prints heading down the old bush track.

'Let's see where they lead' cried a trooper.

'Maybe they are ours from this afternoon'

We followed the tracks, which led us to a creek. One of the troopers stated, 'Hey this is the creek we followed this afternoon, Company is to our left up on the high ground'

'Right' I said 'Let's put the fires out, stay close together and head for the high ground'

We only had to travel about 100 yards, but being pitch black in the jungle you could hear us moving through the bush like a bulldozer.

'Who goes there?' came a voice.

'Private Easterby, 6 Platoon' I shouted.

'What's the password?' came the reply

'Hook in' I stated.

'How many of you?'

'Six including myself' I said.

'Right come in slowly'

We had stumbled upon a company machine gun post, whose gun post it was I did not know or care, I was just glad to have found Company.

The Company Commander (Major) and the Company Sergeant Major (CSM) came down to the machine gun post to welcome us back in as they knew we had been missing for over two hours on a simple clearing patrol.

'Bloody good show' cried the Major.

'Well done' said the CSM 'a good piece of navigation skills'

We took the praise, as I did not have the heart to tell them 'A Tiger made us do it'

I guess my performance, as an acting Lance Corporal on the exercise impressed my superiors as when we returned to the Garrison I was told, along with another soldier to report to the base tailor and collect my first stripe, Lance Corporal Easterby. It was one of the proudest days of my life as I had been in the Army less than two years and now given a type of rank and some responsibility.

Given more responsibility, I no doubt did a lot more map reading and had no trouble in finding my way around in the bush. This is more than I can say for some of the new Junior Officers.

I remember one funny occasion in Borneo, where a Junior Officer insisted that he had arrived at a designated location and was very upset that the Company Commander and the rest of the Company were not there to meet him as planned. The Junior Officer insisted that he was at the correct location and that it was the Company Commanders fault that they had not made contact.

Imagine the Junior Officers surprise when the Company Commander explained to him over the Company Radio, 'Listen you dickhead, turn your map up the other way and get your arse into gear and get back over on this side of the river' Need I say more! Most of the maps we had on Indonesia were not that accurate, however reading them upside down did not help.

On small patrols, I guess I found my map reading quite easy, forget the night clearing patrol. The biggest problem I had with my map reading, like most other troopers, was in keeping count of the paces one travelled. Satellite navigation was not available to the Infantry soldier in the 60's or 70's. Distance travelled and knowing the exact location on a map relied mainly on the number of paces travelled on the ground. Identification of landmarks also helped. So many paces travelled accounted to one mile, or in Army terms 'a click'. One click, one mile, two clicks two miles etc. Each Soldier in an Infantry section was given a turn to count the number of paces travelled while making his way through the bush. You would normally use more than one soldier to count paces as a comparison for accuracy. Each soldier had his own method of keeping count of his paces or clicks travelled. Some tied little knots in string; some collected little stones while others just used their notebooks.

No one liked counting paces, as it was a distraction, especially when you knew there were enemy about, and who knows you could also come face to face with a Tiger. The last thing you would be worried about if meeting up with a Tiger would be counting paces, I know that for me, my paces would be so bloody far apart you would think I had travelled twice the distance.

CHAPTER 5

RELAXATION – PARACHUTING – SOUTH AUSTRALIA/MALAYSIA

All types of sports were available in the Garrison, including rugby against the New Zealanders. I chose a much safer sport, parachuting. I commenced my parachute training with members of the Battalion back in Australia in 1965 prior to arriving in Malaysia. I guess that is where I should start my story.

The Beginning – South Australia – 1965

I have always thought that people who jump out of a perfectly good aeroplane, to hang suspended under a big piece of silk were crazy, until I was given the opportunity to do just that.

While serving with the 4th Royal Australian Regiment (4RAR) in Adelaide in 1965, I helped form a Sports Parachute Club. The club at that time, consisted of all army personnel, however, the club was privately run by the members and had very little connection with the Army. The parachute instructors in the club were mainly ex-Special Air Service Regiment members (SASR), so the training and safety standards set for the club were of a high standard.

During my initial training, I spent half a day in the lecture room, another half day hanging in a parachute harness, suspended from the roof of one of the base warehouses and another half day learning how to land so as not to break a leg or my ankles.

My first big day came one morning at a place called Pinnaroo, South Australia. Our club had hired a Cessna aircraft and to parachute out of the aircraft as a trainee from 3000 feet cost at that time approximately $15:00 a jump. The first eight jumps from the aircraft were to be by static line. A static line jump is where a cord is fitted to the back of your main parachute (tied with string) and the other end of the cord secured to the aircraft. The idea being that when you jump from the aircraft, the cord pulls tight, breaking the string on your main chute so that it is opened for you automatically.

Once you had confidence in yourself and felt that you would have no trouble in opening your own chute, the static line was replaced with a ripcord. The ripcord consisted of a steel handle attached to a steel cable and pins. The pins secured your main parachute so that it did not spring open once packed. Inside of your main parachute was a smaller parachute, spring loaded which when released helped your main parachute to open. On leaving the aircraft you dropped to your designated height, grabbed your ripcord and opened your own parachute. You would then tuck your ripcord down the front of your clothing. Also fitted to the front of your harness was your spare parachute, if for some reason your main chute failed to open or you had problems with your main chute, and had to detach it, you would then open your reserve by hand.

On top of your reserve chute you had two aircraft altimeters. These altimeters would show how far you were from the ground so that you would know when to pull your ripcord. Our club rules were that you opened your chute at a height of 2,500 feet. The reason for this safety margin was to give you time to think and deploy your reserve if your main chute failed to open.

My first jump from the Cessna at Pinnaroo went quite okay, as I did not have a lot of time to be scared. I got out of the aircraft, put one foot on the aircraft wheel and I was away. A few seconds later, I was under silk, gliding to earth, taking in the view while at the same time looking for the cross marked out on the ground and on which to land.

My second jump from the Cessna was different; I had time to think about the first jump and how high I was from the ground. On leaving the aircraft, I lost my stable position (face to earth) and went over on my back. The pilot chute, which deploys the main chute caught around my wrist. While wrapped around my wrist, it was not pulling the main chute from the pack on my back. I was falling to earth. While I was trying to free the pilot chute from my wrist, I was not able to deploy my reserve chute. I fell to within 800 feet of the ground before I managed to free the pilot chute. The main chute opened fully but I had a hard landing!

Before I could decide if I was going to continue parachuting, another chute was strapped to my back and I was airborne again

PARACHUTING – MALAYSIA –1965-1967

It was, not until I had my first parachute jump from a helicopter that I was happy and confident with my stable position and confident enough to pull my own ripcord. By this time I was in Malaysia.

Outside of helicopters, Cessna aircraft and an old DC6, our club jumped out of anything that would get us to 5000 feet, or higher. At 5000 feet an Olympic Size Swimming Pool looked like the size of a third of a match box and an average oval looked like the size of a matchbox.

The two years I spent parachuting in Malaysia with the club certainly had its moments. Parachuting is an experience one never forgets and the feeling of free fall or tracking across the sky is fantastic. Very few sports would hold such thrills.

I had some concerns when parachuting over Terendak Garrison, as when you took off from the base airstrip you flew out over the sea, Malacca Straight. Jumping from 5000 feet over the base you felt as if you were jumping out over the water. Should a strong wind have come up, or some other problem arise there was every chance that you could land in the sea. I was terrified of this as I am not a good swimmer at the best of times.

Another thing is I don't like sharks and I could also imagine trying to free myself in the water with all that silk and lines about me. Because we flew out over the sea and the fact that we were parachuting so close to the sea we wore inflatable life vests. This did nothing to ease my concerns, as there was no gun, hand grenade or rocket fitted to the vest to kill sharks.

One of my experiences while parachuting out over the Garrison was that on one of my jumps I missed landing on the main oval, and landed on the Battalion parade ground instead. To anyone who knows anything about parade grounds, they are as sacred as a cemetery. You do not walk on a military parade ground unless you are on parade, especially a 4RAR parade ground. When you land on a parade ground in a big heap, wrapped in silk it's even worse. Not only that the ground is bloody hard. Needless to say, I spent the remainder of the day sweeping the parade ground with a 1-meter wide broom. Take it from me; a Battalion parade ground is big and even bigger when you sweep it. It was dark when I finished. I never landed anywhere near that parade ground again.

Another day I was parachuting out over a military base near the causeway between Malaysia and Singapore. I had entered a club parachute contest between our club and a group of British Commandos. Our club was competing well, until one of the RAF instructors put our team out of the aircraft into cloud. Once I had dropped through the cloud and opened my chute, I found I was a long way from our drop zone. I landed about a mile from our designated area and to make matters worse, landed on a parade ground full of Gurkha soldiers! All they saw was this big shadow and on looking up saw me about to land on top of them. After interrupting their parade, I landed in the middle of the parade ground on my bum, and knocking the wind out of myself. The little Gurkhas had to pick me up and help me into a rescue vehicle. All the while, all I could do was just grunt as I had no air getting to my lungs and my bum hurt. The parade ground was bitumen and hard as hell. At least I did not have to sweep it. I guess I could consider myself lucky, as my mate fell through the roof of a Gurkha hut and received cuts and bruises.

I believe our worst jumping display was when we agreed to parachute out over Kuala Lumpur, the capital of Malaysia. The display was to open the sports week between Malaysian schools. We were to land in the main stadium of Kuala Lumpur and receive a gold medal from the Malaysian King.

The idea was that five of us were to parachute out over Kuala Lumpur at 5000 feet and land in the middle of the stadium. Another part of the display was to attach a smoke grenade to one of our boots, and while dropping to earth, set off the smoke so that we had colours tracking all over the sky. Even the Cessna aircraft had been fitted with coloured smoke grenades.

Unfortunately, no one in the club had used smoke grenades while parachuting (so we found out later) I had a green colour smoke grenade and when I finished, I no longer had a white parasuit or white face I was all green.

After leaving the aircraft at 5000 feet, I pulled the cord, which set off the smoke grenade attached to my left boot. I was wearing thick leather jump boots and between the boot and grenade I had placed a half-inch thick felt pad. I may as well have had nothing on my ankle at all as the smoke grenade got so bloody hot it burnt me through the pad and leather boot. Unbeknown to me at that time, my mates were having the same problem. I thought at least someone in the club would have tested the heat of the grenades before strapping them to our boots! By the time I had dropped to my safety level of 2,500 feet to pull my ripcord, the smoke grenade was still in full colour and when my chute opened, the smoke began to choke me. At the same time I could not see for the smoke, or where the hell I was, or in which direction I was to drive my chute. My foot was hot, I was choking, I could not see, and I was becoming green.

My only hope was to remove the smoke grenade from my boot. I knew even if I got it off, I could not drop it for fear of killing someone down below. The bloody thing was so hot I had difficulty in getting it off my boot. I eventually managed to free it and drop it further down below me and let it swing on the string I had used to set it off. I was still having difficulty seeing through the smoke.

By the time I could make out a few landmarks and look for the stadium, I was too low to fully make it into the ground arena. I landed outside the stadium in between a large concrete wall, tractor and main street. Only one of the team made it into the stadium and even then he was tangled in his lines and landed on his head. The kids thought it was great anyway. The other three members of the team landed in traffic just outside the stadium. It was one of the most frightening jumps of my life. We all had sore and burnt ankles, and each the colour of our smoke grenades, me green, one red, one orange, one purple and one blue.

Kuala Lumpur is a big city, and to find a small oval in the middle of all that mess from 5000 feet was a bloody miracle. I remember at the time someone saying that we should try parachuting at night. I must have been crazy, then at age 19, what would you expect, young and stupid.

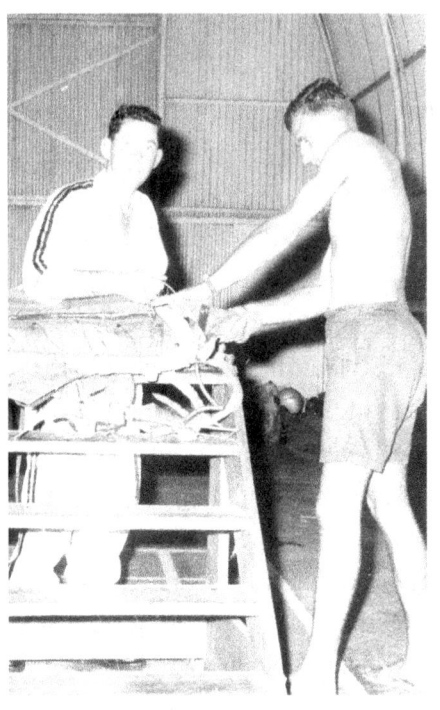

Terendak Garrison, Malaysia 1966-1967. The Author, left and 'Borneo Bob' packing their Parachutes for the next jump.

Both members on board the Army Chopper for their next skydive.

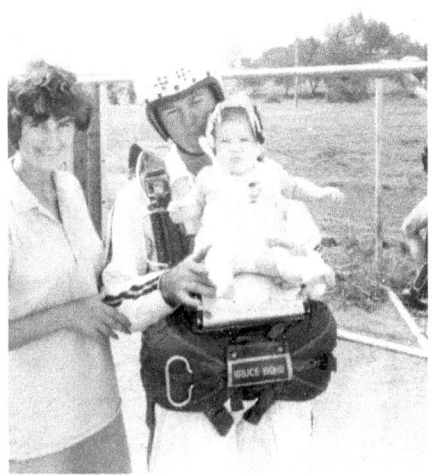

Author with his daughter Tanya resting on the reserve chute.

CHAPTER 6

BORNEO – APRIL 1966 TO SEPTEMBER 1966

'Borneo Bob' and Section members returning from a clearing Patrol outside of the Stass Military Base, Borneo 1966.

The Battalion arrived in Borneo about the 27th April 1966 and was involved in confrontation against the Indonesian Army. The confrontation resulted in large-scale search and sweeping operations, long-range patrols, border crossings and ambushing operations. The Battalion, on arrival divided its four companies up into four separate areas, A Company going to Gumbang, B to Stass. C to Bau as Reserve Company and D Company to Bokah. All areas of strategic military importance.

Troop movement by the Indonesian forces was mainly from the State of Kalimantan, Indonesia. The jungle was thick, with very few roads and a complete mountainous area. The whole area also contained a mass of swamps. Bravo Company was situated very close to the Indonesian border and had its main base camp just outside a small Dyak village called Stass. Stass was in the middle of nowhere, somewhere at the end of a road, which led back to a main town called Bau a few miles away.

STASS MILITARY BASE

Like something out of a movie, such high ground, large bunker systems for as far as the eye could see, all surrounded by barbwire entanglements. Lush green, low vegetation outside the camp made it stand out for miles. Our section bunkers overlooked the large chopper pad area situated outside the camp and on a small ridge.

On arrival at the base we had to rebuild all the bunkers as we had taken over the complex from the famous Gurkhas. The Gurkhas being rather small could stand up in the bunkers they had constructed but when we Aussies went to stand upright in them we had a few problems.

Our beds inside the bunkers were stretchers placed on two levels of timber slats. At night the large shrews (big rats to me) would fall between the slats and end up in your mosquito net with them clawing, you screaming as you tried to fight your way out of bed without hitting your head. At the same time trying to get out between the main beams holding up the roof of the bunker. What a nightmare! The odd krait (poisonous snake) would also make its home between the sandbags in your bunker. It was not uncommon to rebuild your bunker if you saw a snake head appear between the sandbags.

The base was re-supplied by parachute drops once a week and it was not a good time to be inside your bunker when one of the drops missed its target in the outer field and landed on your bunker. I saw many a bunker flattened to ground level. We were all instructed to be outside of our bunkers on re-supply day.

Our beer ration was two cans per man, per night, perhaps. I could never understand how we could spend a month out in the bush and on returning to the base find out that our beer ration had been used. Someone had a bloody good time on our rations and it was not I.

The Battalion had a policy of one month out on operations in the jungle and only two days in camp. The Battalion continued with this policy throughout its first tour of Vietnam. The two days spent back at the Stass base camp each month was mainly taken up with perimeter patrols, re-supply of equipment, clothing, food, medical needs and briefing for the next operation. The section machine gun had to be manned at all times so you were on roster day and night as well. There was never a lot of time for oneself and what time you did manage was taken up writing letters home. There was no place to go for relaxation as the local Stass village was out of bounds unless you were involved in building the new school for the village children. Those who helped build the school were either soldiers on light duties or base staff. The two days in base and the month out on operations became a normal part of life. I think we had two entertainment groups visit the base within the 6 months tour however I was out on operations during both their visit.

MINEFIELD

I did not like walking out of the Stass camp to commence any operations as the only thing between the base and the Indonesian border was swamp and one bloody big mountain. The mountain went straight up into the clouds and took hours to climb. Five minutes out from the base you were up to your armpits in stinking swamp and covered in leeches. Once clear of the swamp, you became a pack mule to climb the bloody big mountain. When you finally reached the top of the mountain you crossed over this narrow track before moving down into Indonesia. On one occasion we found that the track on the top of the mountain had been mined. The Indonesians had turned the top of the mountain into a minefield.

The landmines were not waterproof, which I believe, saved our lives as they had filled with water preventing most of them from working. We only found them after standing on a few which didn't detonate. The anti-personnel mines were a simple device consisting of two small plastic boxes, one box would fit neatly inside the other. Half of the bottom box contained a small piece of plastic explosive connected to a detonator which took up the other half of the box. The top box contained nothing but a small ridge on the inside which when placed over the bottom plastic box lined up with the detonator. The idea being that when placed on the ground you stood on the top plastic box and the ridge inside would crush the detonator which in turn would set off the explosive taking your foot or leg with it. Simple, cheap and hard to detect with a mine detector, not that we had any anyway. Once the detonators had been in water for some time they no longer worked. Thank god for small miracles! Approximately 20 months later I found myself caught in another minefield this time in Vietnam.

We also spent a lot of time getting in and out of helicopters in Borneo as most times we were deployed as a quick reaction force. Quite a lot of the time the choppers could not land because of the rough terrain so we had to be lowered down through the trees by rope with all our gear. That was an experience all by itself.

THE JUNGLE

The jungles of Borneo not only contained human life but beautiful animals, plants, birds and spectacular flowers not seen anywhere else in the world. I remember the Orang-Utans, or man of the forest. according to the Dyaks (headhunters) of Borneo. What magnificent apes, they were as scared of us as we of them. The Orang-Utans are such smart and sensitive creatures. It would have been so easy to have mistaken them for the enemy at times in such dense jungle. I am glad to say none were killed or injured by our presence. We also came across the Proboscis Monkey, what a strange creature with its red face, long pendulous nose, orange top, white collar and grey body. A truly strange primate. The forest contained some of the most interesting species of plants that I have ever seen, I would also have loved more time to have studied the inhabitants other than those that were there trying to kill us.

Besides the animals and other creepy-crawly things in the jungle, you had to contend with the 'Wait-a-While'. This vine was all over the place and consisted of a very fine hanging vine with razor sharp thorns. The thorns faced one way and when you walked into the vine, you had to wait, walk backwards and free yourself. Hence the name 'Wait-a-While'. If you tried to go forward without removing the vine, the thorns would act like the teeth of a saw and cut you to pieces. Many others and I had a lot of respect for these vines.

DYAKS-IBANS

The Ibans of Sarawak, one of the least understood of Borneo's tribal peoples and possibly the most forceful of the Dyak tribes. Referred to as the headhunters of Borneo they have a history all of their own. The

Battalion used several of the local Ibans as scouts to help track down the elusive Indonesian Army. I did not have a lot of faith in the Iban scouts that we had scouting for our company, as when we asked them to comment on signs which had been found, we were told 'Five men, four days' or 'Four men, five days'. The answer was always the same. Maybe it was our Malay. They were lovely people anyway. They remained our forward scouts until they realized that they could step on a landmine or be shot at, so we eventually replaced them with our own troops as forward scouts. My notes also refer to the communal homes of the Dyaks/Ibans, the 'Long Houses' where several families lived together as a community. These large, long, bamboo structures set high off of the ground. What I remember most is the human skulls, which hung from the ceiling of each 'Long House'. We were told that they were the heads of Japanese Soldiers taken by the tribes during the Second World War, some may have been, but the majority were no doubt heads from other tribes, which they had once fought. The Dyaks/Ibans are known to be headhunters, the practice said to have been stamped out by the government but I doubt it.

BORNEO BOB

'Borneo Bob' I shall call him, was and still is a great friend of mine. When we were in Borneo together, Bob was the Number 1 on the section Machine Gun and I was his number 2 on the gun. We were using the Bren gun at the time, which had been converted to fire 7.62mm NATO rounds. The Gun was magazine fed and each magazine contained some thirty rounds of ammunition. Bob carried 15 magazines for the Gun and I carried another 15 magazine's. A bloody lot of extra weight considering I was also carrying 10 magazines of 20 rounds for my own rifle (SLR).

Bob was over six foot tall, skinny as a rake, however loved his food. He would go to great lengths to carry extra rations, including fresh rations, while on patrol. Bob loved to cook and would always start to cook his meal just as the rest of us would be packing up to move on, he never failed. I remember the time in Borneo; we were on the top of this steep ridge overlooking Kalimantan Indonesia. I had just finished my turn on picket on the Machine Gun and Bob was to take over from me. Bob had spent the last half hour making these four small rissoles from a large tin of tuna that he had been carrying for days. The tin of tuna was not part of our Army rations; Bob had purchased the tuna from the Mess or base canteen. This day Bob decided that he would cook these rissoles over his Hexi Stove and that he would use the blade of his machete as a hot plate. After having gone to a lot of effort to cook his rissoles he placed them in a small piece of paper and was about to take over the section Machine Gun when he was spotted by the CSM.

'Tell me Private (Bob) you are not going to eat those rissoles while manning the Machine Gun are you?' said the CSM

'Oh, No sir' said Bob as he threw the rissoles over his shoulder and into the bush. 'No sir not me'

About 10 minutes later after the CSM had walked off Bob was back searching the bush for his bloody rissoles.

I also remember Bob collecting any bits and pieces of Army equipment and Uniform that he came across so that he could exchange the items for new ones at the Company Q-Store. What the bloody hell he wanted so much equipment and uniforms for, heaven knows, maybe he planned to raise his own Army on his return to Australia. I must ask him next time I see him. When I finally managed to ask him, several years later, what he did with all the equipment he collected in Malaysia he could not remember. Seniors don't you just love them.

NATIONAL SERVICEMEN AND THE PHANTOM THONG – BORNEO 1966

It is not widely known that some of the first intake of Australian National Servicemen saw active service in Borneo in 1966.

One late afternoon, in May 1966 the Battalion was reinforced with the first new release of Australian National Servicemen. Approximately 40 National Servicemen and two Officers had been posted to the Battalion and Bravo Company received its share of new recruits. The reinforcements had been brought to Borneo by British Navy ship and some of the ship's crew were to spend a few days in the jungle with us before returning to the ship.

Before I proceed any further, I need to explain a few things. Each Infantry Soldier is issued with a piece of plastic about 2 meters long and about 1 meter wide.

This piece of plastic has a few clips and some eyelets attached. This is your personal tent or hoochie to sleep under and to keep out the rain. As one piece of plastic was never enough to keep out the rain, you joined up with another soldier, clipped his plastic tent with yours and had a bit more cover. Another thing I need to mention is the cords or strings, which are strung around your harbour position, in the jungle, at night so that you can walk around in the dark from one place to the next without falling over. That's the theory anyway! A main string or cord is run from your section machine gun to a central point in your area, you then run your own cord or string from your own tent to the central cord so that when it is your turn to take over duties on the section machine gun at night you can follow your cord to the location of the gun. Each day and night in the jungle the section machine gun, which is your main fire power, is to be manned by at least two soldiers at all times.

Now back to the story…

Our objective that afternoon and night was to carry out an ambush, as a Company, at a known river crossing. The Indonesians had been using the same track and had been crossing over the nearby river via a large log, which had been placed there for easy crossing. The jungle was extremely thick and dense in our area and by about 1700 hours (5pm), with the thick canopy of trees above, you could not see your hand at the end of your arm. Another Soldier, Private Murray (Speedy) who owned the other half of the roof of our tent, and I, had just enough time to oil and clean our rifles and were about to eat our evening meal when the Platoon Sergeant arrived. 'Right you two, I want you to dig a trash pit for the Platoon'. (It could have been worse; it could have been the latrine) As we dug the pit I was wondering how the bloody hell would anyone find it as I was having trouble seeing in the dark to dig it. Good one Sarge. By pitch black we had dug a hole about 1meter x 1 meter x 1 meter. Unimpressed with missing out on a hot meal, 'Speedy' and I settled down in our tent for the night. Having to dig the trash pit so late in the evening and the night closing in on us so quickly we had no idea where the rest of the section members were or where they had placed their tents or cords.

After all the foul ups that night, I guess we were hoping like hell that no one would find us for picket duties. No such luck, by about 0200 hours the Lance Corporal arrived at our tent. 'Right you two, your turn to take over duties on the machine gun, your relief in two hours is over there and to find the machine gun follow this cord' After a series of crashing and banging and 'Oh bloody hell, the trash pit' he was gone. We were left again on our own. 'Do you think he meant us?' said Speedy.

'Suppose so' I said.

After locating my rifle, I climbed out of the tent and proceeded ahead of my tent mate and followed a cord, which I thought would lead me to the section machine gun. I had only travelled a short distance when...

'What the bloody hell, piss off!'

I knew at once my Platoon Sergeant's voice and realised I had trampled all over him and his tent mate, bringing down their tent and knocking over the communications radio. Deciding discretion was the best part of valour, I moved the hell out of there, back along the cord and collected 'Speedy' who was still wandering around in circles looking for something, probably me. Another cord was found and we took off only to end up down the bloody trash pit.

By this time (who cared) the enemy would have long gone, our laughter would have seen to that. Out of the darkness came the Platoon Sergeant's voice 'If I find you mob, you will be laughing on the end of my boot'.

Scrambling out of the trash pit I found another cord and on making my way along it with 'Speedy' in tow, travelled only another short distance, when I came across someone else's hand. After the kicking, screaming and shouting had died down; someone said 'Who are you?'

'Who are you?' came the reply.

'What's the password?'

'What bloody password, no one gave me a bloody password?'

By this time we realised there were six of us all holding onto the same cord.

'What's happening?' I said.

'We finished our watch on the guns about four hours ago and on coming to the end of this cord we don't know who to wake up next or where their tents are or even our own tents, what do we do?'

'Join the clan,' I said 'I suggest you hang onto the cord for a few more hours and it will be daylight, in the meantime I have a gun of my own to find.'

By this time my mate 'Speedy' had gone on ahead and I slowly made my own way along the cord. A short time later, I found my way into a muddy ravine and having lost all balance, fell flat on my face burying my rifle in the mud in front of me.

'Of all the bloody rotten luck, one useless bloody muddy rifle.'

(My words were no doubt more colourful)

Out of the darkness I hear 'You must be an Aussie!'

'How the bloody hell would you know?' I replied.

The voice in the dark turned out to be a Midshipman from the British Ship.

'I was put here manning this machine gun at 1800 hours, (6pm), (Time now 0230 the following morning) are you my relief?' he asked.

'Unless you are on the end of this cord, no' I stated

'What shall I do?' he asked

'Stay there until the sun comes up' I said, as I moved further along the cord.

At the end of the cord, I felt around in the dark and came across the section machine gun and triggers to all the anti-personnel mines we had somewhere out the front of me, in the dark. Something was missing, somebody, 'Speedy'.

'Speedy, where are you?' I shouted.

'Out here on the gun' came the reply.

'You can't be' I said 'I have the gun.'

'Can you feel the gun?' I shouted.

'No but I am at the end of the cord' came the reply.

I was on the gun 'Speedy' was sitting on the end of a claymore mine. He had picked up a cord to one of the mines as he bypassed the gun. We remained on the machine gun until daylight only because to venture away from it would only create more havoc.

In the morning, while walking back along the cord to find the original gun group, I found four new recruits and a Midshipman still holding onto the cord while trying to sleep in a crouched position.

The Platoon Sergeant was up mumbling something about killing the bastard that trampled all over him during the night. As the sun came up and began to warm the area, I could not help but smile to myself and wonder what the enemy thought about all the noise in the jungle last night and what the new recruits and the British Midshipmen thought of their jungle adventure.

Needless to say. I did not admit to treading all over the Platoon Sergeant.

The Sergeant said he found this sole print on his tent and he would match it with someone in the Company. I spent the rest of the day trying to convince him that the sole print looked like a thong print, probably the enemy. However, when he told me there were no six-foot Asians wearing size 8 thongs, I decided to bury my jungle boots first re-supply.

THE WELL – BORNEO – 1966

I remember packing the day before for another month operation somewhere in Borneo. The normal bedding, fresh change of jungle greens, ammunition for my own weapon, ammunition for the section machine gun, eight hand grenades, food, spare battery for the platoon radio, field dressings, backpack and basic webbing. No doubt a lot more gear than I care to remember.

Instead of the usual walk out of the base the following morning we were taken out as a Company by choppers. We had been briefed as to our next operation as a group of Indonesian soldiers had been seen across our borders and we, as a Company were to be used as a cut off group to ambush them should they try and cross back over into Indonesia.

I remember the operation very well as it was to have an effect on me for the rest of my life. It was the only time during the Borneo conflict that I can remember having been put down in a clear rice paddy area by chopper without having to climb down a rope in full gear, to push through the canopy of large trees and jungle. This time it was a landing in dry paddy fields, no mud or swamp and I was dry for the first time at the start of an operation. I remember leaping from the chopper, running across open ground with other members to head for the safety of the surrounding jungle. I did not make it as suddenly the ground beneath me gave away and I was falling, my rifle and hat remaining above ground as I fell. I had fallen into a well, which had not been covered or filled in as the long grass had covered the entrance. I did not see it or expect it to be there.

The next I remember, once overcoming the fright, was that my arms were above my head and my face was jammed in against the dirt wall of the well, my feet could not feel anything under them and hung freely. I was jammed some fifteen to twenty feet down, hanging in the straps of my backpack, unable to move. I panicked and it was the worst thing I could have done. I could not move my arms from above my head and my body weight was pushing me further down the well, with my face pushed further into the dirt wall, cutting off my air.

As luck would have it some of my mates saw me fall and were soon at the entrance to the well and throwing down toggle ropes. I could feel the rope with the tips of my fingers but could do no more.

With enough rope I managed to place it around my wrists and hold on while several of my mates pulled from above. They almost tore my arms from my shoulder sockets and my face was dragged up against the side of the well. Brute force was used to get me out, no time to set up some form of lifting device and to dig me out would have been impossible. Had they not acted as they did, I would have suffocated.

The short time that I was in the well in that position has left me with a mental fear of confined spaces. I cannot overcome that fear or stop re-living the nightmare of being trapped in the well. I am just grateful for the guys that got me out so quickly. Thanks guys you know who I mean.

END OF CONFRONTATION – BORNEO 1966

When our company was not crossing over into Indonesia in pursuit of the enemy it constantly patrolled, and set ambush positions on our side of the border. Bravo Company remained at Stass for the entire 6 months on operations using the main military base. The other three companies A, C and D exchanged positions from time to time. The Battalion lost five good soldiers on operations in Borneo, however, none (Killed in Action) from Bravo Company.

Borneo had to have been one of the toughest areas of military operations that one could experience with its unforgiving terrain, high mountains, thick jungle and numerous deep swamps. The amount of extra equipment, which had to be carried by each and every soldier on operations, was unbelievable. The company received very little re-supply of anything while on operations, especially when crossing over into Indonesia.

Confrontation between Malaysia and Indonesia on the island of Borneo ended sometime in August 1966. The Battalion handed over its operational duties to the Malaysian Army and returned to Terendak Garrison in early September 1966.

Operations in Borneo, like crossing over into Indonesia in pursuit of the enemy were kept top secret until 1996.

Top Photo – Part of the Main Stass Military Camp – Borneo 1966. Above Photo – from the Stass Camp to the Indonesian Border was mainly all swamp and in places quite deep, as you can see. Author.

Borneo 1966. Indonesian Confrontation. The jungles of Borneo had to be the most difficult terrain, to carry our search and destroy operations, that I have ever encounted. Author.

Borneo 1966. When you left the Stass Military Base camp there was nothing but swamp between you and the Indonesian Border.

Inside of a Dyak Long House including all the skulls hanging from the ceiling. The skulls said to be those of Japanese Soldiers killed by the Dyaks during WW2. I would be more inclined to think they are skulls from other tribes.

Dyaks in Ceremonial Dress Borneo 1966 and Dyak village including Long Houses. Note the log stairs leading to each house. The stairs are designed to keep most animals from entering the Long House also helps when the area becomes flooded.

The Author standing outside his bunker, Stass Military Base, Borneo 1966.

Iban Village Borneo 1966 – Local Iban Ladies crushing sugar cane to make rum.

The final product is more than 100% proof as I can tell you from experience in drinking it. Our rum ration of Ghurkha rum, while in Borneo, was quite strong but nothing compared to the local Iban Rum. Author.

'Borneo Bob' and the Author inside and outside their Bunker – Stass Military Base Borneo 1966.

The Author at age 19 sitting outside his Bunker – Stass Military Camp – Borneo 1966.

The Author – age 19, Borneo 1966. Dressed in the Baggy greens and soaked in his own sweat.

CHAPTER 7
RETURN TO TERENDAK GARRISON

The Battalion arrived back at the Garrison in Malaysia early September 1966 and after allowing the troops a short leave, returned to normal duties and field exercises.

Several things changed for the Battalion as trained soldiers were required back in Australia to re-enforce units going to Vietnam. Most of the single regular soldiers who had returned from Borneo with the Battalion were requested to return to Australia to fill the positions. The vacancies left by these soldiers in the Battalion were filled by a new intake of National Servicemen.

As I was now married and with a family (Daughter born in Malaysia) I remained with the Battalion until its return to Australia in 1967.

While still in Malaysia with the Battalion I received my first promotion to Lance Corporal, which I have mentioned. It was also during this period of time that I was required to complete an N.C.O. course for Corporal. I was promoted to the rank of Corporal on my return to Australia.

The final months saw the Battalion continue training with the new National Servicemen in preparation for Vietnam. The Battalion had now been advised that it would be going to Vietnam sometime in May 1968.

The Malaysian Internal security had also eased with the ending of the Confrontation between Malaysia and Indonesia. The Communist Insurgents however were still a problem.

I enjoyed my 2 years in Malaysia with 4RAR, I could not have served with a better Battalion or with such exceptional soldiers and I felt a little sadness when required to return to Australia.

CHAPTER 8

ARRIVAL IN AUSTRALIA AND PREPARATION FOR VIETNAM

On arrival back in Australia the Battalion was sent to Enoggera Army Barracks, Brisbane, Queensland. It was now November 1967 and we were once again preparing for overseas duties.

I purchased a war service home at Chermside, a Brisbane suburb, on my return from Malaysia, however, I saw very little of the home or of my family as I was sent to Canungra Jungle Training Center to help train members of the Battalion for their role in Vietnam. I was now a Corporal and I was to be given a new section of National Servicemen to take to Vietnam. I was fortunate enough to have trained with my new section in Canungra; however, we had less than 6 months to prepare for Vietnam.

On completion of our training at Canungra we accompanied the Battalion on several exercises in north Queensland prior to our departure for Vietnam. Even though only two of us in my section of 10 men were regular soldiers, my 2IC, (Second in command) and myself, I knew then, that I had one hell of a good section. I saw no difference between the National Serviceman and the Regular Soldier, in fact at times I could not tell the difference.

As stated, I had very little home life during the final 6 months in Australia prior to leaving for Vietnam; however, the first of my two sons was born on the 13th February 1968. I left for Vietnam on the 21st May 1968. My daughter was now one and a half years old, my son three months old and with some serious medical problems. It was a hell of a time in my life to be fighting another Asian war.

CHAPTER 9

HEADING FOR VIETNAM ON BOARD AIRCRAFT CARRIER HMAS SYDNEY (THE VUNG TAU FERRY) – 21 MAY 1968

I reported for work at the Enoggera Army Barracks, in Brisbane, on the 21st May 1968, like any other day. I had said goodbye to my wife and my two children that morning knowing full well they were not coming to see me leave for Vietnam on board the Aircraft Carrier, HMAS Sydney. I felt sad knowing that it would be at least a year before I would see my family again. My sisters and sister-in-law saw me board the ship at the Brisbane wharves. I remember lining up on the deck of HMAS Sydney with other members of the Battalion as we sailed out of the harbour.

I would have to say that I spent ten of the worst days of my life on board that old carrier. We were given navy hammocks to sleep in and my hammock, like many others, had no ropes to hang it. When we complained, we were told that there was no more rope available in the store. There were 80 of us in this small room along with our gear and I knew then that there was no way that I could sleep in those conditions. The room was not only stuffy and hot but the pipes all over the roof allowed little room for hammocks. It was obvious that this was not a troop ship and very little had been done to accommodate us. I slept on the floor of the upper deck each night after the Captain of the ship completed his rounds. HMAS Sydney was not designed as a troop carrier, irrespective of how many trips she had made to Vietnam.

We trained as a Company/Battalion on deck of the ship each

day, physical training as well as test firing weapons. The basics like sunscreen lotion were not supplied or available on board for the average soldier therefore I burnt badly along with many others.

As I have stated the old carrier was not designed for the number of people on board, the showers and toilets could and did not cope. Every time I showered I was standing in about 18 inches of dirty, soapy water as the drainage system did not work correctly and the toilets were not much better.

HMAS Sydney was first launched as a Royal Navy ship HMS Terrible (I can believe that) in 1944. She was commissioned into the Royal Australian Navy in 1948. She remained in Commission until 1958 and was recommissioned as a Fast Troop Transport in 1962. Unfortunately in 1975 she was sold for scrap metal to a steel mill in South Korea. A sad end to a wonderful ship of the Royal Australian Navy and no doubt to all those who sailed on her.

The only entertainment we saw on board during the 10-day trip was that of a boxing match between one of our Bravo Company Corporals and the Navy Boxer on board ship. I had saved my rations of beer, managed a front row seat at the makeshift boxing ring only to find that the fight was all over in minutes and that we had to report back for duties. When George, our Company boxer, entered the ring, the bell rang to start the fight; George moved out and knocked the Navy Boxer unconscious.

I asked George later on as to why he did not go a few rounds with the Navy guy and give us some time to enjoy a beer or two. His answer 'The guy might have hit me'. Silly me for asking.

I look back now and smile when I remember the boxing match. George, a Bravo Company Corporal, entered the ring dressed in these oversize Army blue shorts, oversize red T-shirt and an enormous pair of red boxing gloves, while his Navy opponent had on his silk shorts, silk gown, mouth guard, fancy towel, bucket etc. He really looked the part. The bell rang as I said and George knocked the Navy guy out cold. I don't know if the Navy Boxer knew whom he was up against in the ring, but you don't shape up to George Bostock and think that you will walk away.

You still owe me those beers that I missed out on George.

HMAS Sydney – Photos courtesy on board Naval Photographer 1968.

CHAPTER 10
ARRIVAL IN VIETNAM 1968

The Battalion was taken ashore from HMAS Sydney in landing barges. Our Platoon, for some reason only known to the Navy, was dropped some 100 meters from the shoreline. Once stepping from the barge ramp we were in water at least five feet deep. The water was up to the bottom of my chin and I could just keep my rifle above water, everything else was wet. My little Gunner disappeared under water once he left the ramp. All we could see was his green bush hat and the barrel of the section machine gun. Several of the section had to rescue him as the weight of his equipment took him to the bottom of the sea and he was not coming up. We managed to make the shoreline; however, all our personal equipment was wet. A great start to the day. I can only imagine if it had been a tactical assault against an enemy on the shore, the casualties on our side would have been horrific.

Once ashore, we were given a quick supply of ammunition and an even quicker ride by trucks through the Town of Vun Tau to Nui Dat. Passing through Vun Tau you could not help noticing the tree lined boulevards, roadways lined with 'Cyclos' (Small Taxis) and the food stalls at the sides of the road. The local ladies dressed in their distinctive 'AO DAI' dresses also stood out.

I remember looking at Vun Tau from HMAS Sydney as we arrived that morning and again as we drove along in the truck. I remember looking out over the lush green countryside and seeing the low level of grey haze and the scatted dark clouds of smoke in the far background. The war was not very far away and yet I also remember the small fishing boats in the harbour going about their daily task as if nothing was happening. Again the unforgettable smell of Asia only this time mixed with jet fuels and burning jungle.

The Battalion took over from the 2nd Royal Australian Regiment on its arrival in Vietnam. Before leaving Australia 4RAR had been reduced by one company and on reaching Vietnam, two companies of New Zealand troops (V and W companies) were added to form 4RAR/NZ – ANZAC Battalion.

CHAPTER 11

NUI DAT
(PHUOC TUY PROVINCE)

On arrival at Nui Dat my section was given three large tents between 10 of us. Sandbags about a meter in height surrounded each tent, which was already erected and covered in red mud. At the rear of each tent were some trenches, which had fallen into disrepair because of all the heavy rains. Inside the three tents it appeared that the previous occupants had not only left in a hurry but the tents had been ransacked. General rubbish, papers, half eaten fruit cake from parcels from home, old webbing, clothing, broken home made furniture and loads of old ammunition littered the floors of the three tents. It took the section a couple of hours to clean up the mess in the tents and another 3-4 hours hiding behind the sandbags as live ammunition had been dumped in the incinerator along with all the rubbish.

CHAPTER 12
THE SECTION – Vietnam

The ten of us settled in quite quickly to our new surroundings and it was not long before our tents had most creature comforts, good comfortable bed, homemade side tables, hanging space for our clothes and a steel trunk to lock away any valuable items. One of the section members had a Bachelor of Arts Degree and was going through his 'Make love not war' Phase. He said he was a beach bum/surfer when called up for National Service and would return to that life after his tour of Vietnam. Half his luck. The soldier was an exceptionally good artist and it was not long before all our section's military steel helmets, were painted in bright flowers. Once painted the helmets were placed amongst the white painted rocks situated outside the front of each of the three tents. The metal helmets, although issued to each member of the Battalion, were not used by the members or the Battalion. The little green bush hats were most preferred. No protection from a bullet or shrapnel, however, more comfortable than a metal helmet. I guess if we had been ordered to wear the helmets we would have, the Battalion was not one for helmets. I would have been much happier being issued with a flack jacket like the Americans, but the Australian Soldier in the 60's was not issued with flack jackets.

I had my share of individual characters in the section; I won't name them but will tell you about some of them. My trooper with the Arts Degree was a pain in the arse when we were out in the bush, he was worse than the boss, always wanting to know where we were on the map, I was tempted to get him a map and a compass of his own and tell him to find his own bloody way about. I think he did it just to annoy me or to see if I was on the ball. A good kid anyway.

My number two on the section Machine Gun gave me a headache

the first couple of weeks in Nam as he hated carrying the spare barrel and cleaning tools for the M60, especially in the carry bag, nicknamed the 'Golf Bag'. On a couple of occasions we were on patrol, making our way quietly through the jungle when all of a sudden this bloody 'Golf Bag' would come whistling past my head scaring the shit out of me. On taking my Number 2 on the gun aside to caution him about his antics he informed me that he would prefer to carry a full M60 Machine Gun rather than tote the extra barrel. After putting his suggestion to a vote within the section, we ended up with No1 and No2 each carrying a full M60 Machine Gun. May not have suited some sections but suited my troops as they were prepared to carry even more link rounds for the two guns. I know I carried some extra 500 rounds for the two guns along with my own ammunition for my M16.

Another of my troops who I will call 'Sleepy 'had a problem staying awake when we stopped for a short rest while on patrol. I had to watch where I placed 'Sleepy' within the section when we were on patrol so that I could get my messages up and down the section line.

I think 'Sleepy' had a medical problem concerning his ability to dose off so quickly. Anyway we managed and 'Sleepy' turned out to be one hell of a soldier, he not only saved our lives by finding a landmine before one of us stood on it he also raced out during enemy fire to rescue a wounded soldier and carried him back to safety. I had a terrific section, each man a hero.

The Battalion had a policy regarding shaving each day whether in or out of the jungle. I could never understand the requirement for shaving in the bush each day as the smell of shaving cream and aftershave was easy to detect by the enemy. My section were required to shave every day to comply with the Battalion requirements although I think some of them were that young they would take a week to grow bum fluff. I remember during my recruit training I was out bush and one morning decided not to shave. I was 18 years of age and thought I could cover the bum fluff on my face with camouflage cream. On being caught for not shaving by the Platoon Sergeant I was made to carry out a dry shave in front of him, it hurt like hell. I have shaved every day since. Strange how you don't forget certain things. It taught me a lesson; however, I would not have subjected any of my section members to such drastic punishment.

Our first task as a section, after we had squared away our tents, was to help build a new Company magazine to store the Company ammunition. The magazine left for us was a mud hole in the ground and the remaining ammunition was under water and caked in mud. Terrific if we needed ammunition or a re-supply in a hurry. Within a few days on arrival in Nui Dat we had everything in order and started operations in country.

Authors Machine Gunner on left, with the M60 Machine gun, speaking with the Platoon Commander – Vietnam 1968.

Author at the age of 21, Corporal Section Commander – 7 Section ,6 Platoon, B Company 4 RAR Vietnam 1968.

CHAPTER 13

OPERATIONS VIETNAM 1968 – PIGS CAN FLY

All quiet, just another early morning patrol a walk in the woods with Company, only problem being we were in Nam.

My section was at the tail end of a Company patrol, and as we moved silently through the thick scrub; an early morning mist appeared at ground level, you could almost sense that something was about to happen. My sections main duty was to protect the rest of the Platoon from any attack from the rear.

We had not moved very far that morning when all of a sudden a burst of machine gun fire brought us all to our senses. The forward section of the Company had come across some Vietcong sitting down having breakfast, so instead of offering them a few laxatives, opened fired on them with their section machine gun. That would have given them the shits.

Within seconds I looked around to see if all my section members had gone to ground and taken up firing positions, all were on the ground except my (tail end Charlie) the last rifleman, who was running around and around this large tree. 'What the bloody hell are you doing? get to ground and face back down the track' I yelled.

His reply 'I don't know which direction the firing is coming from, but from wherever it is, I want to be on the other side of this tree'.

'Get to bloody ground and face back towards the way we just came'. I yelled.

Word was now being passed back to us from the front that we had made contact with the enemy. The Lieutenant (my Platoon Commander) required my section to carry out a sweep of the jungle to our right and advance forward and make contact with the enemy. The enemy, according to the Lieutenant, were using Small arms fire.

On moving out to our right as a section we had not travelled very far when we encountered a large bomb crater. This thing was enormous, you could not see over it, you could not scale it; you just had to go around it.

The crater, no doubt slowed us down, we were travelling in a different direction for a while before being able to line up for a forward assault on the right of the Company. All the time we were trying to make our way around the crater the Lieutenant kept screaming 'Where the bloody hell are you Corporal? Where are you?'

'Where the bloody hell do you think I am?' I thought to myself.

We eventually got clear of the bomb crater and lined up on the right flank of the Company. I lined my troops up for a forward assault on the enemy somewhere to our front. 'Small arms fire, small arms fire' cried the Lieutenant.

I positioned myself central of my troops with the riflemen to my left and the gun group to my right. The jungle up ahead of us was quite thick with some large trees and thick vines, which made our advance slow.

As we advanced you could hear an unusual type of gunfire, however we were too hyped up to worry, and concentration to our front to locate the enemy was our prime concern.

One of the riflemen to my left had dropped back out of our advance line and when I asked him what he was doing, he said he had lost his smokes (cigarettes) and wanted to go back and look for them. I was in no mood to look for bloody cigarettes in the middle of an assault.

'Small arms fire, small arms fire' cried the Lieutenant.

Advancing further ahead, I noted boughs of trees about 150mm in diameter, dropping down on top of us. The boughs were being torn from the top of the trees in front of us as we advanced, you could see and smell the fresh sap. I thought at the time this was unusual, but my concentration was in locating the enemy somewhere to our front.

'Small arms fire, small arms fire'

On coming to a small clearing ahead of us I could see a body in black clothing lying face down. I halted my troops and we went to ground in the safety of the jungle. I was not going to advance across open ground, there was a body in front of me and I did not know if any of his bloody mates were still around.

The enemy had withdrawn leaving one of their dead behind.

On carrying out a search of the area where the enemy were last seen, I found approximately 30 shell casings on the ground. The shell casings were identified as the remains of ammunition used in a Browning 50 calibre machine gun.

One round of this weapon could kill an elephant. My section and I had been standing up advancing towards this weapon.

After I sat down to collect my nerves and to stop my legs from shaking, I now began to realise as to what had been chopping off the boughs of the trees above us as we advanced towards the enemy. I also had time to think about the unusual sound the 50-calibre machine gun made.

The Vietcong using the machine gun was firing high as we advanced, had he fixed the machine gun at ground level he would have no doubt wiped out my entire section and me along with them.

'Small arms fire, small arms fire'

The Lieutenant stayed quite a distance from me for the next few days after I told him I was going to stick one of the Browning shell cases up a certain part of his body.

'Small arms fire, small arms fire' – Pigs can fly.

CHAPTER 14

NUI DAT – VIETNAM – A FRIDGE FOR THE BOYS

Arrival back at Nui Dat from a month's operation in the jungles of Vietnam was always welcomed. The first shower within a month, good food and a proper bed, was magic. Even though our stay in Nui Dat would only be for two days because of our next month operation. Those two days were like a breath of fresh air.

We normally arrived back at the Nui Dat base just before evening meal, sometimes you had time for a cold shower and other times you enjoyed the evening meal in the clothes you had on and in the condition you arrived in. After a month in the jungle without a wash you could not smell yourself or anyone else who was with you. I remember the fresh cooked bread rolls and the fresh milk most of all. After living like an animal for a month at a time, just being normal was a luxury.

The system in place was that the first night back at the base, from operations, you had off to enjoy yourself, have a beer or two or three, go to the movies or just catch up on some sleep.

At the time I was in Vietnam, I was not a big beer drinker, but enjoyed a beer nevertheless. The ration of beer was two cans, per man, per night, perhaps and as we only had one night free, two cans did not go very far. Most of the lads in my section did not drink beer so I would buy them soft drink in return for their two rations of beer. Soft drink was more expensive than beer at that time. After I had had a decent meal I would make my way to the company boozer, collect my rations of beer from most of my section members, find a quiet corner and drink myself into a drunken stupor. Most of the time I would wake up the next morning sitting in the same deck chair, except that I would have one hell of a bloody hangover. I was 21 years of age and fast on my way to becoming an alcoholic. I am glad it was only one night a month. Today I drink very little alcohol at all.

After I awoke from my drunken stupor the next morning, with my head hurting like hell, I would prepare my section members for re-supply of clothing, food and ammunition for the next operation. You would rotate two of your section of 10 men, so that two of your troops would remain behind in camp, each month, for base duties and to rest them. You would normally have only eight of the ten man team, on operations with you. Sometimes, one of your section members would be replaced by a Medic or some other trooper but not that often. Anyway it was good to leave two of your troops out of operations for a month and to give them a rest, unfortunately as the section Corporal I was not entitled to remain back at the base for a rest.

On the first day back in base from operations and after re-supply you had most of the day, if you were lucky, to yourself. You could go to the American PX to buy a few luxuries or just to look around. You could catch up on some washing, letter writing or just do nothing. The base at Nui Dat was quite big as you could expect and the atmosphere was electric. Aircraft were taking off and landing all the time, choppers screaming overhead and the smell of aircraft fuel kept your senses alive. The heat and the unforgettable smell of Asia also helped.

That night you took your turn on picket, normally on your section machine gun for two hours. The following morning you spent the time being briefed on your new operation, double-checked your gear, weapon etc and by about lunchtime, you moved out of the base to start the new operation. Sometimes you would be choppered out, sometimes taken out in Armoured Personnel Carriers (APCs) or just walked out, depending on the operation.

It was on one such night while I was back in Nui Dat, somewhere and sometime during one of my drunken stupors that I engaged in a conversation with some yanks. The conversation must have included the purchase of a refrigerator or an icebox for my section members. I had wanted a refrigerator or icebox for one of our section tents so that my troops could keep their soft drinks cold. Apparently the yanks had agreed to supply me with a refrigerator the next day for the cost of four cartons of xxxx Queensland beer. Don't ask me where I got the four cartons of Queensland beer from or how I paid for it, as I don't know to this day. Maybe I didn't pay for it, who knows! Anyway the deal was done, apparently, and I was told to expect the fridge the next day.

Consider my shock and the Company bewilderment, the following day when this large twin rotor helicopter arrived over the top of our Company position with this large Refrigerator hanging underneath and the crew screaming over a loudspeaker for a Corporal Easterby and wanting to know where to drop the thing. My head was hurting like hell, I did not remember much or realise what was going on. Needless to say I did not get my refrigerator and spent the remainder of the day working in the sun filling sandbags as a Company punishment for dabbling in the black market.

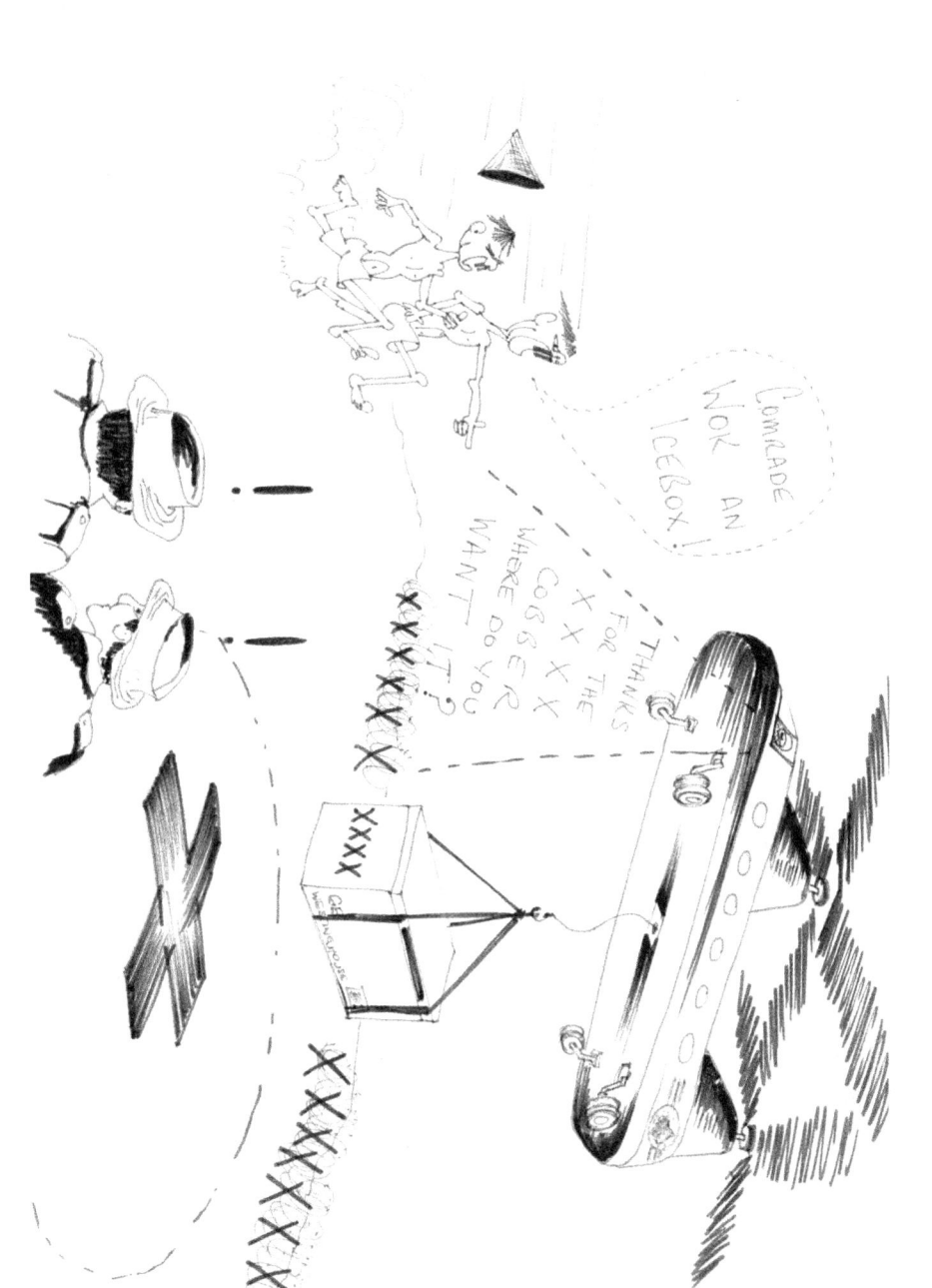

CHAPTER 15

OPERATIONS VIETNAM – BATTALION ATTACK – 1968

This is a story of a Battalion attack carried out by 4RAR/ANZAC after about two months in country. I only saw the funny side of this Battalion attack and this is the side I would like to share with you.

It all started like any other day in Nam, we were on patrol as a Company carrying out search and destroy operations when we received information that one of the New Zealand Companies had located a large force of NVA. The enemy were well dug in and prepared to fight to the end. The enemy had positioned their bunkers between two valleys and in a dense jungle area.

A military decision had been made to hold back a full-scale attack on the enemy until an air strike and artillery strike had taken place. The strikes took place late in the evening, as we were to attack the bunkers on foot early hours of the following morning. I had no objection to the air strikes or artillery strikes, as I did not fancy attacking these bunkers on foot or out in the open like John Wayne.

Early the following morning, about 0500 hours (5am) we were instructed to take up our forward positions in readiness to advance and attack the bunkers. Being pitch black and holding onto each other by rope we moved forward. We had been issued with a very small coloured light each. These coloured lights were used so that we could line up in the dark in single file and in a straight line. If there was any enemy out front that morning he must have thought there was a hell of a lot of glowworms about. I have never understood the tactical use of lights, to help form a straight line. I still do not understand it today. One would think that the most logical thing for the enemy to do would be to zero in on the lights and blast hell out of the area. However, there was not a murmur from the enemy.

Once in position in a single line, we waited until we could see a few meters in front of us. After a short time we were given the order to advance and attack the enemy somewhere to our front. At the same time we were also ordered to fix bayonets. This order, along with everything else, made my hair stand on end and for the very first time in my Army career I was wondering what the hell I was doing, fighting someone else's war. I could not imagine my two sons in this situation. You could say I was pretty keyed up; my eyes were like bloody saucers.

We still had a fair distance to walk to the valley, we were still in thick jungle and the area had not been affected by bombing. As we advanced things became a little clearer as it became lighter. To my left I had four of my own section riflemen, and to my right I had my two-gun group and my two scouts.

Advance was very slow (no one was in a hurry) and concentration was mainly looking ahead and then left and right to ensure we were still in single line. We had not advanced very far when I heard screams to my left, 'SSSSnake SSSSnake'. To my amazement and the rest of my troops, this big tree snake was making its way from vine to vine across our front. Before I knew what had happened, the advance line shattered and there were troops everywhere, obviously like me, they did not like snakes. I spent the next few minutes trying to re-group my troops. Within minutes an explosion to the rear of us took place and some of my troops were hit by flying dirt.

My eyes were almost out of my sockets as we thought we were under attack. The line formed again and we moved forward slightly quicker and preparing to shoot the hell out of the countryside in front. A few moments later, I could hear a scream from my right flank. Someone was screaming about a bug in his ear and someone else was screaming he would get it out with a stick.

As we moved further towards the valley, you could see the forward trenches that the New Zealand troops had dug the day before. I could not help noticing the empty boxes, which once contained hand grenades. I remember thinking to myself, if you needed hand grenades by the box full to attack the enemy, we were in big trouble.

As we moved closer you could see the burnt and scorched ground and the fallen trees. Finally on reaching our objective we came to a grinding halt. What was left of the valley, bunkers and possibly some of the enemy was nothing but fine powdered dirt. The air and artillery strikes had turned the area into fine powder. On reaching the powder, you sank into it like quicksand. We could go no further. I managed to see a dead deer, no enemy.

I was to find out later on that the explosion that took place behind us during the assault was caused by our own troops. Apparently while walking along, one of the troops to my right had got his M79 grenade launcher caught in some vines. Instead of taking his time to free the weapon he used brute force, the weapon discharged and the high explosive went into the air. Some meters from the barrel it armed and exploded on the ground causing some troops to be covered in dirt. Thank god it was not one of my troopers.

The bug in the ear of one of the troopers was drowned at a later date by the medic who filled his ear up with oil. The trooper obviously did not take too kindly to his mate's offer to get the bug out with a stick.

So ended the Battalion 4RAR/ANZAC attack.

CHAPTER 16

OPERATIONS VIETNAM – BRAVE SOULS

Rain, rain, always the rain, it turned the country into a mud hole. Along with that, the Viet Cong had tied us up pretty good by having us patrol by day, and ambush by night.

On one operation my section was in a forward position along the firestone trail protecting the bulldozer drivers (17 Construction Squadron) from being killed by the Viet Cong. You had to admire the dozer drivers, they were there to do a job and to them 'Charlie' (VC) was just another stump who at times got in their way. The only protection that the dozer driver had was a metal helmet, flack jacket and a 9mm pistol. I saw them with little else to protect themselves and they were an easy target for 'Charlie' using a (RPG) Rocket Propelled Grenade.

It was our job for a week, during daylight hours, to position ourselves forward of the dozers and look out for 'Charlie'. One section member would protect our rear and let the remainder of the section know when the falling trees got close and for us to move on. The idea was to clear a strip of jungle 200 metres wide of all trees/vegetation, suitable for a killing field. Helicopters would patrol the strip day and night and anyone crossing over the strip, who was not supposed to be there, were quickly and effectively dealt with.

Funny how at times your eyes can play tricks on you – as it was on one of these land clearing operations that I thought I saw a silver/grey haired man with a dark face looking at me from the top of a large boulder. I got the complexion right anyway. I was so convinced I was looking at this fellow with such silver/grey hair that I asked the lad behind the machine gun if he had seen any of the local people with striking silver/grey hair. He said 'No, why?' I said 'Because there is one looking at me from that boulder up there on the high ground'. What made it worse was that I had placed a sentry out about the same distance, but further to the left of the boulder. When I indicated the area to the machine gunner, the silver/grey haired figure disappeared and it was then I realised it was 'Charlie' (VC) in full camouflage. The smooth shape of the rock had shown up his movement

The boulder was at the end of an old rubber plantation and the dead leaves on the ground made a noise when stood on. You could hear 'Charlie' crawling away at a great pace towards the other side of the hill. It would have been easy to have fired a grenade over the boulder and pick 'Charlie' off, but somewhere out there I hoped I still had a live sentry.

I could not believe that the sentry had not heard or seen 'Charlie' move into our area and observe us.

I screamed at my troops that the enemy were to our front and ran up the hill after 'Charlie' with a few members in tow. We arrived at the top of the hill only to see 'Charlie' and his mates disappear into the deep jungle.

After all these years, I can still see this silver/grey haired man look at me from the top of the boulder, our eyes meet, we check each other out and he fades away. Scary, isn't it?

At night 'Charlie' would slip in and plant landmines at the end of the land clearing operations so that the next day the dozer and driver would become his latest victim. The solution to this problem was to ambush 'Charlie' at night when he came in to plant the mines.

It was on one such rainy night while setting an ambush for 'Charlie' that I had my first section member wounded. A series of mistakes led to him being shot, not by 'Charlie', but by the Platoon Commander's Batman. I don't blame anyone, I would have asked for an inquiry if my own burst of automatic fire had hit its target. I could have killed the

Platoon Commander's Batman had he not gone to ground after firing his shots at us and hitting my trooper.

We moved into our ambush position at the end of the land clearing operation. Our first mistake was that by the time we reached the area, we only had a few minutes of daylight left. Our second mistake was to set up an ambush in an area that had not been cleared of all the fallen timber/vegetation.

Another problem was that the rain had not eased, and to make matters worse, the Lieutenant split us up into two separate sections. One full section moving out to take up a position somewhere to our front across the other side of the fallen logs. By this time I was asked to spread my section on the ground between the fallen logs and to place my gun group (2 men) on the top of a large pile of logs/sand. The best we could hope for was to run our night cords between each other for some means of contact and roll up in our plastic tents to try and keep out the rain. Some of my troops decided to get down into some dozer tracks, in the sand, which were quite deep. However, after a while, with the constant downpour of rain, the holes filled with water.

The Platoon Commander, Radio Operator and Platoon Commander's Batman took up a position forward and at the base of the pile of logs and sand.

My gun group was on the top and above them on the mound. As an ambush position, bloody awful with troops everywhere; no clear fields of fire, an accident waiting to happen. Come nightfall, no one knew where the next person was. The best anyone could hope for was to find someone at the end of the night cords to relieve you after 2 hours manning the machine gun.

It seemed no time at all, the rain had eased and all of a sudden all hell broke loose. I looked over the top of the log from where I had taken refuge for the night only to be met with incoming tracer. I heard a scream, someone say the enemy is in between us and more tracers came my way. The tracer was coming from an area to my front. My own troops were behind me and to my right. It was then I decided to return fire and opened up on automatic with my M16.

Thank God, after firing his shots at us, the Platoon Commander's Batman had gone to ground, for I had put a burst of fire at the centre I last saw the tracer. If the Batman had remained standing, I believe I would have hit him.

As it happened, between the rifle fire and screams, we were getting nowhere. I decided to fire a flare to light up our position. It was when the area became as bright as day that we saw each other and our positions. If the enemy was out there, he was long gone. The bloody confusion between us would have scared them to death.

It turned out that 'Charlie' had managed to crawl in between our two sections, not knowing that we were there. It was easy with all the fallen logs. Even then, we could not have done much for fear of hitting the other section to our left or our front. We had no idea where they were in the dark.

On finding out that the enemy had somehow managed to crawl in between the two sections to plant their landmines, the Platoon Commander had directed his Batman to notify me personally. However, on leaving his position and in the dark, lost his bearings and walked forward of our ambush position, possible towards the enemy.

Realising he was walking in the wrong direction; he did an about turn and walked back towards my gun group. It was said the Batman challenged one of my gun group who was standing at the time and did not hear him. The next anyone knew was that the batman fired at my trooper standing next to the machine gun.

We were later to learn that at least four shots had hit my trooper and that one of those shots hit him behind the knee of his right leg and brought him down. A painful wound with a 7.62mm round. At least three other rounds had touched his clothing, one across the front of his shirt and another two through some items he was carrying in the map pocket of his trousers. Some would say he was lucky, but a 7.62mm round behind your knee will leave you with a disability if not taking off your leg.

The rain started again and the heavy downpour made it difficult to talk and move around. We were approximately 8000 yards from base and no helicopter or armoured personnel carriers were coming to our aid. We were to carry our wounded mate out over the fallen trees/ vegetation.

Initially we were to make a stretcher to carry him out, but to do that we needed light and it seemed pretty silly to be running around with torchlight trying to cut down poles for a stretcher. A decision was made to take turns and carry our mate out on our shoulders. I remember we all took turns to carry him along with his backpack and rifle. For a young lad with such a terrible wound to his leg and who was being carried back over difficult terrain at night and on someone's shoulders, he made very little sound. Takes some guts, don't you think?

It took us a few hours to reach base, my trooper lived, but will remain a cripple for the rest of his life.

I was to spend the next two days in the Regimental Aid Post as I had hurt the base of my spine while helping to carry out my wounded trooper. Another two days were spent on light duties before returning to full duties. Some thirty years later the damage to my spine was to cripple me. It would seem that I had damaged the base of my spine and the back of my neck during one of my parachute landings. I had actually crushed my spine in the fall and was not aware of it until it started playing up a few years later.

Approximately two months later I was to have one of my section members (KIA) killed in action. Blue was my forward scout for most of my time in Vietnam. I will remember my little red haired mate for the rest of my life.

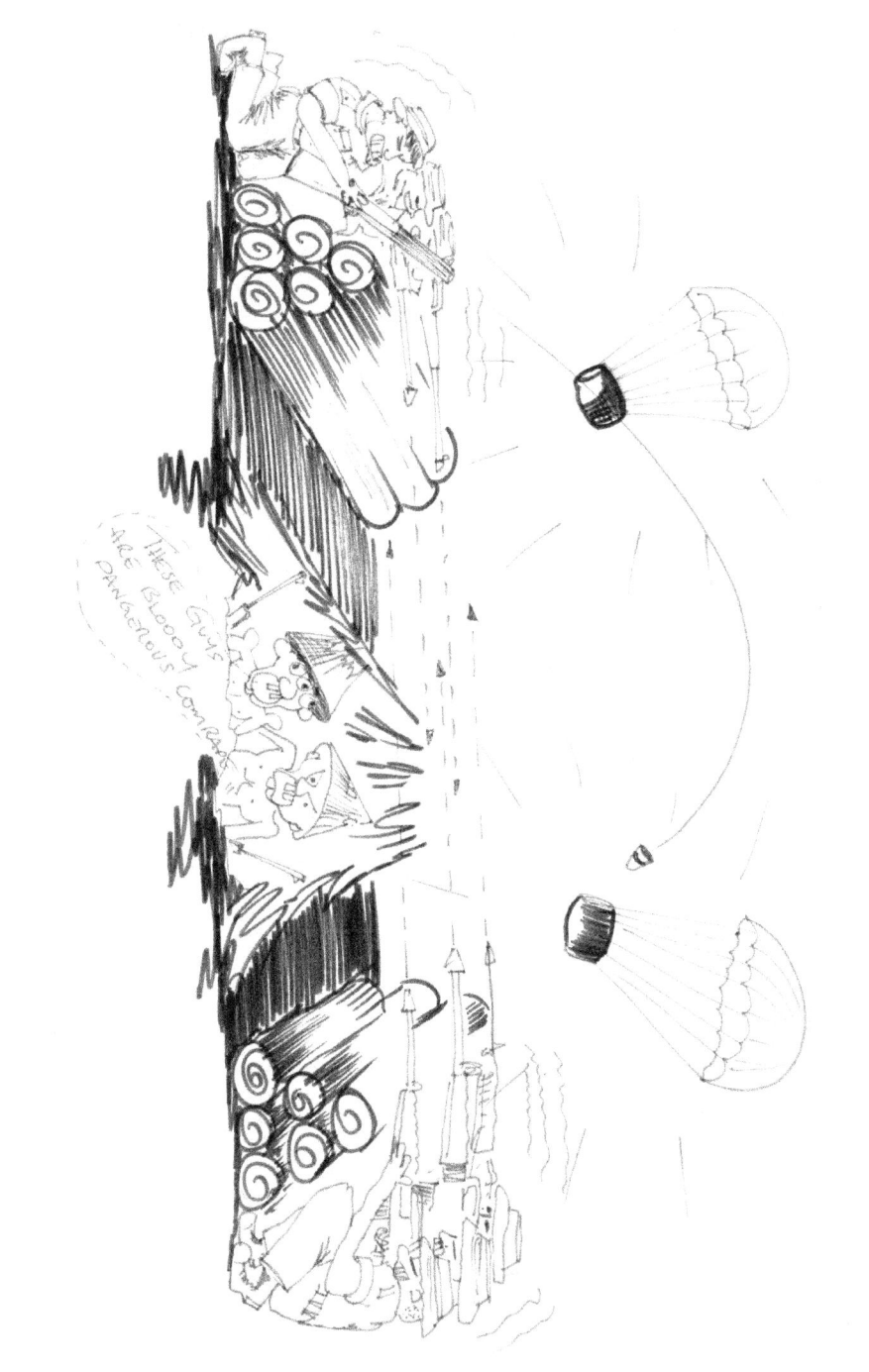

CHAPTER 17

FRIENDLY TROOPS – VIETNAM – 1968

We had received our normal re-supply of food, clothing, and ammunition and had been briefed that morning on our new operation. The whole Battalion was to be moved by Armoured Personnel Carriers (APC's) to a Fire Support Base from where we would carry out search and destroy operations deep into enemy territory.

As an Infantry Soldier, I did not like being cooped up in an Armoured Vehicle, they were hot, noisy and the enemy could hear you coming for miles. Landmines made one hell of a mess of an APC, its crew and us, its passengers.

I can't remember a time when we reached our objective when travelling in an APC. It seemed that every time we reached a paddy field the APC would become bogged. The APC's were an asset to the Infantry Soldier in a conflict but to get us from one part of Vietnam to another part, via the rice paddies, forget it.

This was such a day in Nam, as the APC's bogged down we were told to continue to move to our objective on foot. As we moved towards the thick jungle I was requested to move my section towards the front of our Company and to take the point. Not long into the patrol we received a message via the Battalion that there could be friendly troops operating in our area of patrol. No description of friendly troops, just friendly troops. Hell they could have been anyone. I suppose if they did not shoot at you then they were friendly, what a stupid bloody message!

Just as we were pondering the wisdom of 'friendly troops' my two forward scouts came upon a roadway, and we called a halt deciding to stay within the jungle and observe the roadway. While I was advising the Platoon Commander as to the reason for our stop, my two scouts saw a Vietnamese male and two small boys walking along the road each carrying plastic bags over their shoulders.

One of my forward scouts told the Vietnamese to stop; however, they just kept on walking, waving and smiling as they went. My scouts asked me if they could open fire on the Vietnamese if they did not stop. I said no as I was still struggling with the term 'friendly troops'

As the three Vietnamese males neared a bend in the road just up ahead they dropped their plastic bags and ran off. By this time the Platoon Commander had moved up to my position to observe what was happening.

A short time later, my section moved out of the jungle and onto the road to inspect what the Vietnamese had been carrying in the black plastic bags. The bags contained rice and ammunition, obviously for the Viet Cong.

My section had now taken up defensive positions at the side of the roadway, covering both directions, while the Platoon Commander and one other were searching through the black plastic bags. In the meantime I walked over to talk to the Platoon Sergeant who was standing in the middle of the roadway, all by himself.

Within seconds, all hell broke loose, I heard the sound of an M16 rifle and I was gone. The roadway had an embankment either side about a meter in height and my little machine gunner was in front of me as I leapt from the roadway into the jungle. Unfortunately for the gunner he did not move fast enough as I left my boot print in the middle of his back as I scrambled for cover. The Platoon Sergeant by this time was alone in the middle of the roadway talking to himself.

What had happened was that once the Company had come to a halt, a Viet Cong soldier had tried to sneak up and shoot the Company Commander. Unfortunately for the Viet Cong and lucky for the Major, one of the Bravo Company Corporals saw the Viet Cong first, and fired at him with his M16. The Viet Cong escaped leaving a blood trail but because of other commitments by the Company, was not followed. It was said that the Viet Cong was found the next day by an Armoured Division, 2000 yards from where the Corporal had hit him. The M16 rounds had hit him in the back and he carried what remained of his stomach some 2000 meters before he died. To make matters worse for him, it was said that he had tried to shoot the Major with a French (one shot) musket. So much for 'friendly troops'.

CHAPTER 18

A MEMBER OF WHERE THE F..K ARE WE TRIBE – PART 2

VIETNAM 1968

The second and last time I had trouble with my map reading was on a patrol in Vietnam. I experienced one of the hardest map reading tests of my career. I was to learn later that the maps we were using of a particular area were not that accurate.

I was given the job, along with my Section, of leading our Platoon on a search and destroy operation during the day. We were also to stay out overnight as a Platoon, set a night ambush and return to Company the following afternoon. The distance to travel was some seven or eight clicks before locating our ambush position.

The area of travel consisted of a type of long pampas grass well over 2 meters in height. The pampas grass was sharp, thick, tough and had to be cut down with a machete, the going was tough. Because of the thickness of the grass, the area was incredibly hot, and each and every soldier was given a turn up front to cut his way through. We did not count on the amount of time we would be surrounded by this pampas grass and of the amount of water each man would use during the day.

As you can imagine, asking your troops to count paces while being both physically and mentally exhausted took its toll. Within approximately two clicks (miles) we were no longer that accurate with our paces, and I could no longer count on knowing my exact position on the map. To make matters worse, the Lieutenant kept asking me every half hour as to where we were. I would close my eyes, take a stab with my finger on the map and say 'About here sir.' The Lieutenant would reply 'Very good, carry on Corporal' and would move back to the centre of the Platoon.

I was hoping desperately to locate open ground or find a tree that I could climb so that I could take a compass bearing on some other feature other than the thick pampas grass. No such bloody luck, no trees, high ground, open ground or any other distinguishing feature, just endless pampas grass. The heat was unbearable, we were drenched in our own sweat and our water was running low. How much more each man could take was unknown, there was also heat stroke to consider.

Where was the bloody rain when you needed it? 'Where are we now Corporal?' asked the Lieutenant. 'About here sir.' As I stabbed my map hoping like hell I was within half a click of our correct position. 'Very good' and back he would go to the centre of the Platoon. This went on all day, the only time I managed some peace was when we stopped for a meal break for about 30 minutes. Not that anyone felt like eating surrounded by all that grass and heat.

By late afternoon we cleared the pampas grass and you could see the relief on the face of each soldier, mine being no exception. We had entered into a dry plateau area but according to my map we were supposed to be in a type of swampland. No bloody swamp within miles. I may not have known exactly how far I had travelled but I had never varied from my compass bearing. There was no way I had missed the swamp. If there had been a swamp it had dried up with the dinosaurs!

As I was explaining our position to the Lieutenant we heard Tank movement over towards our left flank. It was an American Armoured Division. 'Head in that direction', Said the Lieutenant, pointing towards the tanks. 'And let's see who they are.'

As we cleared the jungle, we came across a roadway to our left (no bloody road on my map) and I thought where the hell are we? I could not be that far out in my navigation. The maps we were using appeared hopeless. However there was a chance I had made a mistake.

I moved along the side of the roadway and with the Platoon in tow, made my way up to the first American Tank. As I approached it, I saw two guys sitting on the tank turret eating a meal from china plates.

'Hey guys, where the hell are we?' I called, as we were a few feet from the tank. With this, the two yanks did an about back flip, sending food, knives and forks everywhere!

'Jesus man, you scared the shit out of us, where the bloody hell did you come from?' screamed the two surprised soldiers.

'Australia, last time I looked' as I burst out laughing.

The Yanks weren't impressed when I asked about their sentry.

'What sentry?' they asked.

That would be right I thought to myself, sitting on top of a battle tank, in the middle of the road, being able to see for miles and they didn't see a bloody Platoon of 30 men walk up to them. There was hope for me yet.

When we compared maps and grid references, the only thing we had in common on the maps was our starting point, leaving Company that morning. Everything else was different. Their map had the roadway, which we were on, and our maps had no roadway at all. We might as well have been operating in a different country. You would at least think that all allies would be using the same maps, no bloody wonder we were having trouble moving from point A to point B.

As dusk was approaching fast, it was agreed between our Lieutenant and the Officer-in-charge of the Tank unit that we would stay with them for the night and take up a harbour position on one of their flanks.

I kept asking the Lieutenant 'Are you sure these wackers will remember that we are alongside of them and not shoot the shit out of us if someone farts during the night?' 'It will be okay' assured the Lieutenant.

We moved into a harbour position as a Platoon, ran out our night cords to each of our machine guns and settled down for the night. We had been instructed to dig a shell scrape (trench) each in case we came under fire during our stay, the only trouble being that we were over solid rock in most areas. My little machine gunner managed to dig himself quite a deep pit so that when he lay flat in it he was just below ground level. My shell scrape consisted of an outline marked over solid rock; hopefully we would not need the pits. Wrong again.

It would have only been a couple of hours after nightfall and I guess we were astounded as to the noise made by the Americans alongside us. I thought for a while that we were in Club Med. Why anyone would want to use so many torches and start moving a tank around in the middle of the night, I don't know. These guys were bloody crazy. I was hoping like hell that they didn't decide to drive the tank forward in our direction, and praying that the Lieutenant was on the radio reminding them of our position.

The first mortar round fell a few hundred meters out and for a while we did not know what was going on. You could hear the mortar but the noise was not coming from the American compound.

We were later to learn that the Americans had given away their position and were about to be mortared by the Viet Cong.

I don't know how many rounds fell on our position but you don't want to be around tanks when they fire at ground level over your head. We could not hear a thing as the ringing in our ears took care of that. I think most of us were wishing that we had dug a hole in the ground to crawl into and I guess a few of us remembered the hole our little gunner had dug. The little gunner was not impressed when four of us tried to get into the hole with him.

Next morning we could not leave the Americans quick enough, finding we were all intact as a Platoon, it was time to head back to Company.

The Lieutenant had decided that we would go back the same way that we had come the day before, back through the pampas grass and again my section was chosen to lead the way

The heat of the day, the long grass and again our water running low. The Lieutenant still wanting to know where we were every half hour. About lunchtime the Lieutenant advised me that the Company had now moved to a new location and that I was to set a new compass bearing so that we could meet up with the Company before nightfall. I could not believe my ears, here we were again surrounded by pampas grass, not able to see more than a meter in front of us and I was to change direction on a new compass bearing. Bloody marvellous, I wished for once I was in Club Med.

During the afternoon the Lieutenant kept asking 'Where are we now Corporal, how much longer until we reach Company?' 'We are about here sir' as I stabbed my map with my finger. 'As for meeting the company, that will depend on how much more pampas grass is around us and if I can get some help cutting our way through'

By dusk we blundered out into an open clearing, we were completely and utterly exhausted. Just as I was about to take up my bearings we heard the sound of metal being banged together and I told my forward scout to head in the direction of the noise. We walked right in on one of the Company sentries, god it was good to be home.

The Company Commander came out to meet us as we ushered our weary troops through the Company position, the Lieutenant, my Platoon Commander, paused and in front of the Company Commander stated 'An excellent piece of navigation there Corporal, well done'

If only they had known that for two whole days I was no bloody soldier, but a genuine member of the where the f..k are we tribe.

Next time I would ask the artillery for a smoke round to help mark my position on the map, however, knowing my luck, I still would not have been able to see the smoke above the pampas grass. On second thoughts I think I would be better off at Club Med.

CHAPTER 19

THE PLASTIC BULLET – VIETNAM – 1968

Talk about embarrassment. We were choppered into an area in Vietnam called Bien Hoa. The Battalion was to relieve 'Mike Squad' an ARVN (Army of the Republic of Vietnam) Ranger Unit that had suffered heavy losses on search and destroy operations in the area

True to our training, when we jumped from the American choppers we went to ground and took up defensive positions to protect the aircraft and ourselves. Only problem being we were dropped off into open rice paddy fields. I was not impressed as within minutes of the operation, I was lying up to my armpits in stinking water, mud, leeches and some other long worms, which could have been eels or snakes. To make matters worse, when I looked to my left, the unit we were taking over from were all standing on solid dry ground in their pretty Tiger Suits looking at us Aussies rolling about in the mud like local pigs.

We spent a month on operations in Bien Hoa. Our search of the entire area, which was pretty thorough, did not result in our Company coming under any heavy enemy contacts, only an embarrassing situation for me.

While carrying out a search of a particular area one morning, my forward scout came across two Viet Cong who were using the side of a track as a toilet. One fellow had his pants down and being in a crouched position steadied himself with his rifle. The other soldier was talking to him while enjoying a cigarette; his rifle was slung over his shoulder.

As we were a reasonable distance away from the two Viet Cong and concealed in the jungle, the Platoon Commander said that he did not want the enemy to escape, and that I should use the M79 grenade launcher on them instead of trying to shoot them. I called on my rifleman, who carried the grenade launcher and who was the best shot with the weapon, to take out the two Viet Cong at the side of the track. I had seen this rifleman put a grenade from this weapon into a bucket 200 meters away; he was good, that was why he carried the weapon.

Only a couple of days before, I had spoken to my ace rifleman with the grenade launcher and told him to replace all his canister rounds (buckshot) for the weapon with high explosive rounds. About 10 minutes after I had told him to replace the canister rounds he came back to me stating 'I got rid of all the canister rounds Corporal, we have nothing but high explosive rounds for the weapon'. Nothing more was said and I forgot about the matter. The reason I had asked the lad to replace the canister rounds with high explosive rounds was that I believed the canister rounds were useless in the type of conflicts we were involved in. Unless you were standing on the enemy the buckshot was useless.

Now back to our two Viet Cong at the side of the track. In the company of the Lieutenant I instructed my ace rifleman to use the grenade launcher on the two enemy to our front. 'No problem Corporal' and as he took aim we waited in anticipation.

BOOM! And as the smoke and dust cleared, all I could see were these two Viet Cong running up the road like hell. One guy leaving his rifle and pants behind while the other guy about ten paces in front of him. They ran that fast they were out of rifle range within seconds.

What had happened was that my ace rifleman with the grenade launcher had replaced the entire canister shot with high explosive rounds all right, except for the one in the chamber of the weapon. The hardest thing to hit the Viet Cong sitting at the side of the track was the big piece of black plastic in the top of the round. I was not impressed and neither was the Lieutenant. I bet the two Viet Cong went out and bought lotto tickets.

We finished the month in Bien Hoa without further incident. The enemy must have decided to wait until we left the area as when 'Mike Squad' returned they suffered heavy losses once again.

CHAPTER 20
LANDMINE – VIETNAM

It was a Battalion policy not to use jungle tracks, and as a Company we had been walking all day in the jungle alongside a major track when we stopped for a short break.

While we were stopped, a Vietnamese woman with a baby at her breast walked along the track and observed us. It was normal policy to check out the woman and any other local people and send them back to our base to be interviewed. As night was falling it was decided not to give our position away any further by calling in a chopper, let the woman and child continue on their way, and set up a night ambush along the track.

The night passed uneventfully, other than for heavy overnight rain, which soaked our clothing and turned the area into a mud hole. That morning the Company was informed that it had to be at a certain location by a certain time and to hurry things along we were to use the track which we had been walking alongside the previous day.

I was busy burning the leeches from my body, which I had collected overnight while lying in the ambush position when the Lieutenant came up and advised me that our Platoon would be leading the Company to the new location and that my section would take the lead or point duties.

As I only had 8 men in the section on operations, instead of the normal 10, I sometimes had to cut back on having two forward scouts. In this instance I had one of my riflemen, who was also our section medic and ace shot with the M79 grenade launcher, take over forward scout duties. I had used this section member because I had been kicking him up the bum for the past week for looking at his feet as he walked along instead of looking further ahead. I kept saying to him 'Sleepy, if you don't lift your head as you walk along, all you will ever see are the feet of the man that shoots you.' By putting 'Sleepy' up the front and as my forward scout gave me a chance to get him to lift his head, either that or he would have my size 8 boot up his bum.

I don't believe we had travelled more than 600 meters along the track when I was about to sink my boot up 'Sleepys' behind, that was until he stopped and called me forward.

In the middle of the track and on the ground was a leaf with a piece of sticking plaster attached to it. Next to the leaf, buried in the ground was a hand clacker used to set off a claymore mine. The clacker had been buried upright in the ground with the leaf stuck to the top to hide it so that it could be stood on to detonate a mine. The overnight rain had washed the leaf from the top of the clacker; exposing it 'Sleepy' had noticed it while staring at the ground.

An Engineer (Sapper) was called forward and he located a 9-inch diameter homemade, Viet Cong, anti-personnel mine placed within an anthill at the side of the track. The anthill had been scraped out overnight and the mine carefully placed inside the termite mound. The mud on the outside of the anthill had been carefully replaced and packed so that it looked like the original anthill mound, clever little buggers the Viet Cong.

It became apparent that the woman with the baby that we allowed to pass through our Company position the previous night, instead of sending her back to be interviewed, was obviously Viet Cong or working for the Viet Cong. I believe she gave away our position and set us up for the landmine, hoping that we would use the track.

The Engineer blew the landmine, which exploded, like a large bomb. Had 'Sleepy' not been looking down at the ground as usual, one of us would have set off the landmine and several good soldiers would have been lost.

Thanks Soldier you saved several lives that day!

CHAPTER 21

TYPICAL DAYS IN THE JUNGLE – VIETNAM

The noise the rain made pouring through the overhead canopy of trees was almost like standing beside a roaring waterfall. We had been lying in an ambush position for several hours and found concentration becoming quite difficult, you needed to go to the toilet, as well as fight off sleep. I was watching the leeches crawl all over my body, and in and out parts of my rifle. The more it rained the worse the leeches had become. I was worried they would get to places on my body undetected, and leave itchy sores which they had a habit of doing.

My jungle green uniform was now black in colour, stained by dirt, sweat and mud. The back end of my trousers were pinned together with safety pins from my field dressings as the stitching had rotted away. Another few days and my clothes would literally fall off of me. The cleaning kit for my rifle was in a similar condition, as the cord used to pull the oily rag through the barrel of my rifle had rotted and broken away. I had no other means to clean my rifle other than to borrow someone else's cleaning kit.

We normally had good re-supply and equipment exchange while in the jungle, but most of our re-supply was still in Australia sitting on the wharf. The wharfies had decided to go on strike in connection with Australia's involvement in Vietnam. I don't care what their gripe was; we still should have received those supplies. I reserve my thoughts on this matter.

Ambush positions are difficult at the best of times, as you still need to go to the toilet and stay awake. If you went to sleep in an ambush position there is every chance you could become the one taken by surprise. We spent a lot of time setting up ambush positions both day and night, some successful while others fairly mundane.

Every aspect of our infantry training was put into practice on each and every operation. The time you lacked concentration was when you were taken by surprise. If you went more than one or two days without a contact, I found that each day after that you became a little more careless. You had to keep reminding yourself as to where you were, and ensure that you passed that message on to the rest of your section members. They might not have liked you for it at the time, but if it saved their lives or the lives of their mates, so be it. We were all there to do a job and my section, along with the rest of the Company, did it well, I was proud to be part of the team.

My own greatest fear was what I could not see, and that was landmines or booby traps. I was prepared to fight the enemy on my terms but mines and booby traps were another issue. I had survived, after walking into a minefield set up by the Indonesians in Borneo in 1966. I was not prepared to walk into another minefield in Vietnam, this time one set up, not by the enemy, but by the American Army. As a foot soldier, irrespective of rank, I was never made aware of any minefield areas set up by friendly troops other than outside of a base perimeter. I doubt if the Company, let alone the Battalion, were notified of any friendly troop minefields, there were no minefields marked on any of my maps.

The minefield that we blundered into as a Platoon was in an area, which had been mined by the Americans by dropping the mines from an aircraft. The mines had been dropped over a large area to help stop enemy movement. How these mines worked, I don't know, only that once they were on the ground, they were activated and would explode when walked on. My section was sitting down taking some time out for a meal when we noticed these yellow plates on the ground around us. One of my section members had been sitting on one of these plates while eating his meal. Looking around further we found several more of these yellow plates, which turned out to be landmines capable of blowing a person in half. Why they had not exploded when stood on, I do not know, we were not staying around to find out. It took us several hours to prod the ground and to find a safe way out of the minefield.

Another time my Section and I were sent to a creek to fill water bottles for the Platoon. I remember crossing the creek to take up a firing position on the opposite bank. As I made my way up the steep embankment, I came face to face with a 9-inch diameter Viet Cong anti-personnel mine. The mine had been made out of ration tins left behind by the American Army. I had seen these mines before, they were packed with high explosive, broken glass and pieces of metal. What had saved me was that there were no Viet Cong around the place to detonate the mine. On checking the area further, I found that I was standing in the middle of a very well camouflaged Viet Cong bunker system, overlooking the creek. The bunker system was not that old, and it appeared that the previous inhabitants had left in a hurry. I was beginning to feel that I had nine lives. We blew two mines, which we found in the area, it was unusual for the enemy to leave the mines behind and not booby-trap them.

CHAPTER 22

FINAL PATROL – VIETNAM – 25th August 1968

The smell of the green crisp jungle, the rays of the sun passing through the canopy of trees above, it seemed a perfect morning as I had a few moments to enjoy a cup of coffee and time to reflect on how far we had come as an infantry section in Vietnam. We had survived several conflicts after 5 months in Nam along with a minefield, several booby traps and a mortar attack. Of my section of 10 men, we had lost one killed in action and one wounded. I had promised a lot of mothers that I would return their sons alive and all in one piece. A hard promise to keep while serving in Vietnam.

That morning I had been directed by my Platoon Commander to take out a small patrol and locate a new campsite for the Company. We had been in our current location for about four days, and by carrying out constant patrols by day and ambushes by night, the enemy were sure to know of our camp location.

I was tired; I had been on a long patrol the day before, part of an ambush team that night and I had two large infected leech bites on my right thigh, which were making my life miserable. While on patrol the day before, I tried to jump a small, deep stream, but because of the weight of my backpack I missed landing on the opposite bank and entered the water. If it were not for my section members, I would have drowned, as I had no way of getting out of the water by myself .The weight of my backpack took me to the bottom of the stream. It was not the first time that they had saved my life.

As I had spent most of the day soaking wet after my near drowning, I failed to notice two or more leeches that had stuck to my right thigh.

They must have had their fill of me during the day and fallen off as I found two big fat leeches inside the bottom of my trousers, that afternoon. The two marks left by the leeches on my right thigh became infected and were like two large boils. What was making it worse was that my basic webbing was rubbing up against the infected sores. Had I not been asked to take out a patrol that morning I may have had time for the Platoon Medic to have inspected them.

My section of eight men, including myself, and a wireless operator moved out of the Company base by about 0900 hours. Our mission was to locate a new campsite for the Company. I was to look for an area close to water, an area which gave us plenty of cover and above all an area which would allow a re-supply by choppers.

The trip out from base and on foot was slow. I had two members scouting ahead of me, a signalman behind me, a machine gunner on the left flank, another machine gunner on my right flank and the rifle group bringing up the rear. We were a band of 9 men, alone and in Vietnam.

We were to travel light and as fast as possible, each man was to carry one meal, his basic webbing, ammunition for his own weapon and no backpack. Each man, including myself, was also to carry a minimum of 200 link rounds for the two M60 machine guns.

As we were only 9 men I was instructed to avoid contact with the enemy if possible and to pull back if we ran into any trouble. I knew I was in range of our artillery support but at that time I was not aware that we would have no chopper support for any casualties.

About three hours out from our Company base we came across an open, flat area to our right (north east), some old dry rice paddies and to our left (North West) a heavy wooded/bamboo area. Parts of the bamboo area were quite thick so I decided to check out the area and move away from the open ground. The open ground would serve as a chopper pad area.

On moving in to take a look at the wooded area, we came across a fresh water creek and on moving further in, came across an old Viet Cong bunker system. The style of the old bunkers and junk left around the area indicated that they were Viet Cong and not Task Force construction. Fortunately for me I decided to put the main body of my section behind solid cover (large fallen log) and had two of my troops check out the bunker system.

At the base of some bamboo trees we could see several, old china rice bowls. The bowls were half full of bamboo shoots, which I estimated to be several hours old as they had withered and discoloured. Thinking that the enemy may still be close by, I urged my troops to be careful, especially when checking the bunkers. Booby traps, as well as the enemy were our main concern.

After being given the 'all clear' concerning searches of visible bunkers, I took my map and compass and walked out with one of my scouts towards the open paddy fields. The main group, including the radio operator were to remain behind the large log. On the other side of the large log the area was open and had been cleared of all vegetation and to be caught out in the open by the enemy would be disastrous.

As I moved out towards the rice paddy area, I placed my compass on top of my folded map to get my true compass bearings and at the same time placed my M16 in the crook of my arm. My scout was behind me and to my left.

On moving closer to the open area, a small foot track was found with an irrigation ditch running alongside and on the left of the track. To the right of the track, I observed a rather large tree stump about two meters in diameter and about a meter above ground. As I walked towards the tree stump, I got the shock of my life as the grass at the base of the stump moved and a young lad stood up and fired at me point blank range.

The lad was dressed in dark clothing and had on a coolie hat covered in grass to blend in with the surrounding area. The weapon he had in his hand was small with a perforated outer barrel and had a small circular magazine.

The lad was obviously a Viet Cong soldier and as he open fired; I brought my rifle forward into my hands and pulled the trigger. I thought at the time that I fired, I was facing him, however I was later to realise that I had been blown backwards about two meters and onto my back. I felt I had been hit by a big gust of wind. Looking at my rifle while still lying on my back I saw that I had a shell casing jammed in the ejection opening. When I pulled the trigger of my rifle I must have already been on my back and the angle of the rifle caused a casing to jam it open. By this time all hell broke loose as shots were coming from every direction.

My scout had gone to ground in the irrigation ditch and I managed to roll in behind the tree stump. At the same time the lad had disappeared, not staying around to finish the job. I was alive and I felt no pain and I thought for a moment that the lad had missed me. It was when I tried to stretch out behind the tree stump that my left foot felt cold and wet. On looking down, half of my shirt had been blown away and the link rounds I had been carrying as bandoleers across my chest had also disappeared. I was later to realise that the two bandoleers had taken most of the impact with only one bullet penetrating my left flank. The cold wet feeling in my left foot was my boot filling with blood. I then saw what were my intestines hanging out of the hole in my left flank and then I began to hurt.

Information from the remainder of my troops, who were behind the log, indicated they were caught in a crossfire and could not move away from the log. At the present time I was on my own. Every time I stuck my head round the tree stump someone took shots at me.

Knowing that I was a bleeder at the best of times, I had to stop the bleeding and fix the wound. If I passed out due to the loss of blood, I would probably die. The will to live was quite strong; the sight of my intestines poking out through a hole in my body did nothing for my piece of mind. I had to fix the wound and get back to my main section of troops. I managed to place two field dressings over the wound but the pain was unbearable, tears kept clouding my eyes and I could hardly see.

Eventually I managed to crawl across the track from the tree stump and roll into the irrigation ditch. The incoming fire was heavy and I had no time to look or try to return fire. My scout was hugging the bottom of the ditch for all it was worth and I don't blame him, like me he had nowhere else to go. The two of us eventually managed to crawl back along the irrigation ditch and join the main section behind the log. Unfortunately, like the remainder of the section we could go no further than the log. Anyone trying to move away from the log would come under heavy fire.

What had happened was that the enemy were still in the area, and dug in under the bamboo. Almost impossible I know, but there they were. Not using the old bunkers but new and better ones. The bamboo above the bunkers was better than concrete, impossible to take out with anything we had available at the time. Every time we stuck our heads above the log to try and locate the enemy we took in immense fire.

I ordered the group to spread out as best they could and use hand grenades on the suspect areas. Having eight hand grenades each we blew the area to pieces, however, as we closed over the slits in the bamboo from where we were taking fire, you could see sticks being used from inside the bunkers to re-open the holes. We seemed to be in a no win situation. If we stayed much longer we ran the risk of running out of ammunition, if we tried to leave someone else could be killed or wounded.

The radio operator had managed to notify the Company of our position and was told that reinforcements were on their way, unfortunately no choppers were available at the time and the reinforcements were coming on foot. I knew we could not hold out until help arrived, as we were three hours out from Company. The only other help available was artillery.

We managed to get the first artillery round on the ground within fifteen minutes, which was pretty good in Nam. The first round was a fair distance out, but we eventually directed the fire right in on our position. Our idea was to try and crawl out under the artillery fire and once clear blow the place to pieces. We placed the two M60 machine guns to our rear to cover our withdrawal and we slowly crawled clear. Once clear we instructed the Artillery battery to flatten the area.

About half way back, while heading towards base, we met up with the reinforcement section who said that they would check out the area once the Artillery had stopped. It was hard to believe that when they went into the area the Viet Cong were still there. I believe it was not until the Viet Cong heard the sound of choppers that they decided to withdraw from the area.

On searching the area after the Viet Cong had departed an elaborate bunker system was found along with some food and traces of blood. No bodies were found as most of the time the Viet Cong took their dead with them if they had time. According to the Corporal in charge of the reinforcement section my section had struck a group of Regular Viet Cong Soldiers and not just a guerrilla group. That was probably why they had stayed so long and put up such a fight.

I remember reaching our old base on foot and the Company Sergeant Major coming out to help me in. After that I guess my body gave up, as I don't remember anything clearly until waking up in the hospital at Vun Tau the following day.

God was smiling on me the day I was wounded in Nam, the impact of the rounds fired by the young lad were taken by the machine gun rounds that I had wrapped around the top of my body. I was left with a bruised and purple stomach for a while and the one round that did penetrate passed through my body without damage to any of my vital organs. The two infected leech bites had to be lanced to remove the poison. For a while I had to lay flat on my back with both my flanks hurting like hell, a small price to pay, I was happy to be alive.

CHAPTER 23

THE ENDING OF MY ARMY CAREER

I spent 11 days in the hospital at Vun Tau after being wounded. On my return to Nui Dat I was informed that I would not be able to return to active duty, as it would take some time for my wound to heal properly, I was going to be sent home. I will always regret the decision to return home as I felt that I had let everyone down.

I was also very bitter at being brought home in civilian clothing, in civilian aircraft, through the back door so to speak, along with other wounded. It would appear that the Government of the day did not want to draw attention to the dead or wounded coming home from Vietnam. I still remember the funerals, Guards of Honour in which I was involved in while stationed at Terendak Garrison, Malacca, Malaysia. The soldiers that were buried in the Garrison Cemetery during my time had been killed in Vietnam. It was only later on that those Australian Soldiers killed in Vietnam were returned to Australia.

On my return to Australia, I was given a short break (8 days) before being posted to Canungra Jungle Training Centre as an Infantry Instructor, to train more troops to go to Vietnam. It was during the short time I spent at Canungra that I found I was having back problems, not being able to carry a backpack or to have any extra weight pressing down on my spine. It was also during this time that I realised I was having some mental problems, which were not going away. The Army sent me to a Psychologist, which I now know, was a waste of money, as the guy had no idea what was wrong with me. According to him I had a bad childhood, sound familiar? The guy was not on the same planet as I had a terrific childhood, growing up with loving parents, three older brothers and five older sisters all of whom loved their little brother. It was not my childhood that was worrying me; I think it had something to do with three Asian wars.

I left the Army on the 13th December 1968, taking an early discharge.

After a few more trips to the Psychologist and after having punched up several members of the class for calling me a baby killer, I felt I could no longer rely on medical help. The class that I was placed with consisted of alcoholics and drug addicts, nothing of which I suffered from. I think the saving grace for me at that time was that after leaving the Army a few months after returning from Vietnam, I was given the chance to work my father-in-laws farm in Balaklava, South Australia. I lasted two years but spent those two years by myself, each day, operating a tractor.

I look back on my Army service, the comradeship and the excitement that went with it. I have asked myself many times as to what makes a good soldier, especially an infantry soldier and was I a good soldier? I came to the conclusion that if you are the type of person who does not like going without sleep, sleeping wet, does not like going without a shower or bath or like having your clothes rot off of you, then I was not a good soldier.

I have also thought, what if, I was given the chance all over again to serve in the Australian Army with those jungle green pack mules, those giants among men, would I? BLOODY OATH I would and be proud of it.

CHAPTER 24

TRANSITION – ARMY – RAAF

After leaving the Army in 1968 I moved with my then wife and two children, to a farm in Balaklava, South Australia. I was no farmer however I was given the opportunity to work my father- in- laws farm. My father-in-law was in his senior years and had no sons to work the farm.

I was quite prepared to learn and work the farm even though I knew nothing about farming or farm animals.

Unfortunately from the start I had problems as I could not lift anything heavy because of my sore back. At the same time I was suffering from severe Post Traumatic Stress Disorder of which I was not aware, even though I was being seen by a Psychologist.

The two years that I spent on the farm was not to my liking. I worked 364 days a year refusing to work on Christmas Day. I put in 1000 acres of wheat/barley on our farm and worked another two share farms. We also had sheep, cattle and pigs to look after.

My marriage was falling apart, while we were on the farm, I will not go into detail for the sake of my children. I decided to leave the farm with my two children and return to my War Service home in Brisbane. I had worked the farm for two years and left without a cent to my name.

Two months after returning to Brisbane, my then wife decided to return to the family home. I went back to earning a living as a Spray Painter, which was my trade before joining the Army.

I felt out of place in Civilian life and wanted desperately to return to Service life. It was then I decided to apply again for the Services but I was still having trouble with my back and my temperament was not improving.

It was in June 1971 that I filled out an application to join the Royal Australian Air Force as a RAAF Policeman. I declared my back problem and the fact that I had been seen by a Psychologist after leaving the Army in 1968. On the 13th August 1971 I was accepted as a candidate for the RAAF.

CHAPTER 25
BRIEF HISTORY OF THE ROYAL AUSTRALIAN AIR FORCE POLICE (RAAF SERVICE POLICE)

Reference: Courtesy RAAF Police Association webpage, 2005

The role of the RAAF Service Police/Provost Unit from 1930 until 1981.

The role of the RAAF Service Police/Provost Unit is to prevent crime and to provide police and security services to the RAAF at all locations. This responsibility covers physical, personal and intelligence security and involves:

1. the investigation of offences associated with the RAAF
2. the investigation of matters of a compassionate nature involving members
3. counter intelligence investigations
4. the maintenance of off base discipline
5. the provision of RAAF and security guards to protect VIP aircraft
6. the provision of advice to commanders on special police matters
7. including physical security, control of entry to bases
8. traffic and crowd control
9. the efficient use of police and security guards, and
10. the conduct of character and security vetting.

The Provost Services within the RAAF began in a very small way during 1930 when service police were first established for unit duties. The first Provost Marshal and Assistant Provost Marshal were appointed towards the end of 1940, but it was not until 6 April 1942 that the RAAF Service Police Unit was properly established and organized. The headquarters of the Service Police Unit was formed in Melbourne with detachments in each State and overseas.

The service was reorganised as the RAAF Provost Unit from 16 January 1961, with Sections in each State except Tasmania and North and South Sections in Queensland, all reporting to Headquarters in Melbourne. Commanding Officers of the Provost Detachment Units were known as Assistant Provost Marshals.

In March 1979, the Unit was renamed the RAAF Police Service. Organizational change within the Unit, however did not become effective until 1 September 1979. At this time, the Unit relinquished control of RAAF Police Offices throughout Australia, with State offices coming under the administrative control of RAAF support units in the respective capital cities. HQ Support Command Unit in Melbourne, and Base Squadrons in both Townsville and Darwin.

On 12 February 1981, Headquarters RAAF Police was disbanded. Command Police Offices were established within the two RAAF Commands (Support Command and Operational Command) in 1981, to assume the quality control function for RAAF Police Offices under their respective Commands. At the same time the previous agency was relocated to Canberra, and became known as RAAF Police Records Centre.

The role of the RAAF Service Police/Provost Unit from 1961 until now

On 16 January 1961 the RAAF Provost Unit was formed, establishing a Headquarters in Melbourne, and Detachments in Victoria, New South Wales, South Queensland, North Queensland, Northern Territory,

South Australia and Western Australia. Specialist sections such as; Special Investigations Branch, Field Security, Port Detachment, mobile patrols for traffic duty, street patrols to ensure good conduct by troops, and Compassionate Section were formed.

On 22 November 1962 the RAAF Provost Unit provided security for His Royal Highness the Duke of Edinburgh. The duties included security guarding of the RAAF Royal transport aircraft, crowd and traffic control and security duties associated with the royal tour. Duties since that tour have included security and traffic duties, guarding of all visiting VIP and Royal aircraft, security for President Lyndon B Johnson, President of the United States and guarding of His Royal Highness, Prince Charles and his party and all aircraft associated with that tour.

On 22 December 1967, No 14 Security Guard Course began at 7 Stores Depot Toowoomba and graduated on the 24 April 1969. On the 12 December 1969, 33 Basic Service Police Course graduate from RAAF Base Point Cook. Up to 1978 many courses were conducted including the Advanced Service Police Course, Investigators Course, Drug Investigation and Field Security Courses.

The RAAF Service Police were raised in March 1979 and the RAAF Provost Unit was disbanded on 1 September 1979. At the same time, control of RAAF Police Offices was handed over to the Support units at the nearest RAAF base or establishment. Headquarters RAAF Police was disbanded on 12 February 1981.

1982 saw the formation of the Defence and Security Training School (currently the RAAF Security and Fire School)

The Police Dog Training Centre Toowoomba 7SD was renamed the Security Guard Training Flight and became Detachment A.

In 1986 the Security Guard Training Flight was moved to RAAF Base Amberley where it became the Police Dog Training Centre. Traditionally the RAAF employed "Police" dogs for the sole purpose of security. While this type of dog could track using 'wind' scent, it was generally aggressive to strangers, and predominantly used on foot patrols, alone, out of hours. On the flight line. While reasonably effective in a benign security environment, these dogs were not considered suitable for use in GRDEF OPS. In 1996 a project team was formed to assess the capability of Military Working Dogs (MWD), in particular, working with GRDEF in the Patrol and Surveillance Area (PSA), Close Approach Area (CAA) and Close Defence Area (CDA)

In 1994 the RAAF Police Dog Handler, RAAF Police and RAAF Police Investigator mustering's were amalgamated into RAAF Police. In 1996 the RAAF Police mustering was renamed RAAF Security Police (RAAF SECPOL). The formation of the Information Warfare Cell (IWC) and Physical Security Cell (PHYSEC) occurred in1996. Since 1945 RAAF Service Police have served overseas in all theatres of war, as well as UN and peace keeping missions; including Korea, Malaysia, Thailand, Vietnam, the Sinai, Cambodia, East Timor, Afghanistan and Iraq. The transition from Service Police to RAAF Police in 1994, when Dog Handlers were amalgamated with investigators and General Duties personnel, and then Security Police in 1996, brought with it huge change, with the emphasis on Force Protection (FP) rather than Law Enforcement (LE).

The following information brings us up to date as to where the RAAF Police are today.

INFORMATION COMPLIMENTS OF RAAF NO28 (CITY OF CANBERRA SQUADRON INFORMATION CIRCULARS)

Thursday 4 July 2013 will mark a significant day in Air Force history. The disbandment of the Security Police (SECPOL) mustering after 18 years of service and the establishment of the Air Force Police (AFPOL) and Air Force Security (AFSEC) mustering's signal a critical step toward creating the required Security Forces workforce for Air Force

2020. 4 July 2013 will also celebrate the establishment of three new Security Force Squadrons that will integrate the entire operational Air Force Security Forces workforce.

Any incident mentioned in this book that you

think refers to you is purely coincidental,

surnames have not been used to protect the innocent

along with possibly some of the comedians.

To write about humour in a Police role is difficult however I

have tried my best and I apologize if you think

any part is considered derogative, as it is not intended.

I feel sorry for people who cannot laugh at

themselves, especially if it makes one happy.

CHAPTER 26
ENLISTMENT AND TRAINING WITH THE RAAF

I joined the RAAF on the 13th August 1971, in Brisbane, Queensland. Prior to being accepted as a candidate for the RAAF, like everyone else, I attended an interview and sat for several tests.

I remember the interview that I attended in connection for, the then "Service Police" Mustering. One of the questions that I was asked was, 'Did I have any friends that were Policemen, either Civil or Service?' I said that I knew a Civil Policeman who attended my local church. I said that I only knew him as 'Felix' I called him Felix the Cat, not to his face of course. I never thought much more about the interview. Little did I know that everything that I had said in the interview was thoroughly investigated, and my friend Felix, was interviewed as to my Character. Imagine my embarrassment in church the following Sunday when Felix came up to me during the service and let out a thundering 'Meoooooow.' Be careful what you say during an interview.

I was accepted into the RAAF; however I had to go, once again, through recruit training, as I had been out of the Army for just over two years. I did not mind going back through Recruit Training as I knew nothing about the Air Force or the RAAF Police. I spent several weeks doing my basic training at RAAF Base Edinburgh, South Australia. I was on course 1129. I learnt all the basics once again, marching, weaponry, rank structure and trained with a great bunch of guys. I had a fairly easy time as I was still fairly fit except for the pain in my spine. The drill had not changed however I thought the Army was a lot better at it. The Rifle that I used for drill had not changed, the SLR, (7.62mm Self Loading Rifle). I came third on the course, beaten academically by some of the younger recruits. I had left school at 15 to go to work so I was not embarrassed. I was Course Orderly the entire time of our training and by Graduation Day had taught the remainder of the Course members how drill and marching should be done. I left RAAF Base, Edinburgh as Aircraftsman T. Easterby, Service Number A122073. Just another Serviceman.

RAAF Recruit Training Course 1129 – RAAF Base Edinburgh, South Australia, August 1971. Above – Author, front row, first right. Below – Author, second row, third in from right.

CHAPTER 27

RAAF BASE WILLIAMS, POINT COOK

The home of the Royal Australian Air Force, Point Cook was established in March 1913 as the location for the Central Flying School, and was in continuous operation as a flying training base from 1914 until 1992. Point Cook has also been home to Officer Training for the RAAF since 1947, as well as housing a wide range of other activities. (Extract from RAAF Museum, Point Cook)

After leaving RAAF Base Edinburgh, I was posted to RAAF Base Point Cook, Victoria in October 1971. There I was to do my basic training for the Service Police, as they were then known. I had to wait until January 1972 before my course started; therefore I was attached to the Base Service Police Section for on the job training. I was very fortunate as one of the Corporals who I will name "Jock" would instruct me during the week on every aspect of police work and then he would have me sit a written test the following week, on what I had learnt. I appreciated his help very much and respected him immensely. Jock went on to become a Provost Officer. By the time I commenced my Basic Police course (number 39) I had a much better idea of what was expected of me. As I had my family with me and close by, in a Caravan Park, I was fortunate enough to live away from the base during my course. I would stay on the base if I felt I needed extra time to study. I enjoyed the course very much and the company of the seven other trainee Service Police members. I was also fortunate enough to work again with four of the course members, several years later. On completion of the course all members were promoted to Corporal and each given our postings. I was told that I was going to RAAF Base Laverton.

*Service Police – Basic Training Course No 39 –
RAAF Base Point Cook, Victoria.
April 1972 – Author, rear rank, first left.*

RAAF Service Police Basic Training Course No 39. How not to handle a drunk driver. By allowing him to run away.

CHAPTER 28

RAAF BASE LAVERTON – VICTORIA

On completion of my Service Police course in April 1972, I was posted to RAAF Base Laverton, Victoria, just a few miles down the road from Point Cook. I now had the rank of Corporal which is the rank given to every Service Policeman or Woman, on completion of their course. I was also given a black and white, felt, armband with the letters SP attached. This was to identify the wearer as a Service Policeman/woman within the RAAF. I was right back to the rank that I had obtained in the Army, serving as a Section Commander, in an Infantry Battalion. I felt quite at home.

RAAF Base Laverton was a large Operational Base during the time I was there. My duties included Investigations, Security Patrols and general Police duties. My boss, a Flight Sergeant, (two ranks higher) was a hard task master, as within a week I was expected to know the names of all the streets on the base, where all the intersections were and what every building was used for. I found the RAAF a lot different from the Army, the rank structure was similar but that was as far as it went. The camaraderie side of the service was not the same; there was a huge gap, probably because of the type of job. Your only close friends seemed to be other Service Police and their families. As Service Police we were referred to as "Screws" by the average Airman. I did not think much about it as it did not worry me. I just assumed that any Service Personnel, who had been caught doing the wrong thing by the Service Police, would no doubt believe that they were hard done by and were being Screwed.

I took my job seriously, acted fair and worked alongside other

Service Police just as dedicated. I will not go into any of the serious investigations that I was involved with during my time at RAAF Base Laverton. I saw the Service from a Policeman's perspective, something the average RAAF member or Public does not see or sometimes hear about. Any serious offences committed within the service were normally investigated by the Service Police in company with the Civil Police or Federal Police.

RAAF BASE – LAVERTON

The main subjects of this book are about the humorous side of the Service, so that is where I will start my stories involving RAAF Base, Laverton. The incidents that I do remember are in no particular order or dates as we are talking about some 35 years ago and I do have my senior moments. My memories concern an Officer on the Base, who I believe, meant well but was a real pain in the arse. He was not a Service Policeman but as we had no Provost Officer on the Base, he was, never the less, responsible for our Administration.

It was about two days after the members on the Base had been issued with the new RAAF uniform. The new uniform consisted of a light blue shirt, dark blue tie, dark blue trousers and a matching dark blue jacket. This uniform replaced the original Khaki polyesters which you will identify in several of the early photographs, contained in this book. The only times that the polyesters were again worn as a RAAF uniform was when you served in the tropics, like Darwin or Malaysia. In summer you could remove the jacket of the new blue uniform, allowing you to wear a long sleeve blue shirt or short sleeve. A nice uniform, smart, but the suit jacket was not much use in winter as it did not keep out the cold. One thing springs to mind, whoever tested this uniform prior to it being adopted by the RAAF, did not spend his or her time on an open Air Base, in the middle of winter, especially in Victoria. Thank god for the Flying Jackets Tarmac Jackets.

Back to our story, I was working a night shift with another CPL Service Policeman, we were still getting used to our new uniforms as it was bloody cold and we were in no hurry to leave our warm office to go on either a foot patrol or mobile patrol. We had not been issued with a Flying jacket or a Tarmac jacket at the time, as wearing of these two types of jackets was still a contentious issue. Pilots wore Flying Jackets and only members working out on the Tarmac were issued with Tarmac Jackets. Everyone else wore the new blue uniform coat. No consideration had been given to our Police mustering working shift work, on Air Bases. As there was only two of us on duty on the night shift only one would patrol while the other manned the police radio. We both took it in turn to carry out security patrols of the base during our shift. It was about 2300 hours (11pm) when in through the doors of the Guard Room, at a great rate of knots, came Officer Blogs. (To me public enemy number one) This member outranked us of course and insisted that he was going out on Mobile Patrol. The member required my offsider to accompany him; however he (the officer) would drive the Police vehicle. As the Officer was entitled to go out on patrol and drive the Police vehicle, we were in no position to refuse his request. Our Service Police vehicle, at the time, was a Kombi Van, fitted out with a blue flashing light, Police radio and a wire cage in the back which was used as a lock up for wayward Airmen. If I had known what was about to take place I should have locked the Officer in the bloody cage.

The Officer was advised that night flying was in progress on the Base and that he should not go anywhere near the Airfield, without first obtaining clearance from the Base Tower. The last I saw was the Kombi being driven up the road at excessive speed with the blue light flashing. I knew then it would be an interesting night. I was to learn later that the member at the wheel was only going to the Canteen to purchase cigarettes. My offside no doubt suitably impressed.

Two hours passed and I was not receiving any response to my radio calls to the Police vehicle occupants. Had an emergency arose on the

Base I had no transport to attend and as I was in charge of the shift, I had to answer for the use, time and mileage of the vehicle. I heard nothing but crackling sounds on the radio.

It was about 1.30 am when all of a sudden the main doors to the Guard Room burst open and there stood the Corporal covered from head to toe, in wet, red mud. His new uniform, a mess. The Corporal was also swinging a large piece of wood and at the same time screaming, 'Where is the bastard, I'll kill him.' You beauty I thought, my first murder investigation.

After I managed to calm the Corporal down, he explained as to what had taken place. I was informed, contrary to our advice; the Officer had entered the Base Airfield and drove straight down the centre of the strip without Tower approval. On reaching the end of the runway he ran off the end and managed to bog the Service Police vehicle. Unable to free the vehicle from the mud, the Officer then ordered the Corporal to get out and push, while he increased the revs. After a time the vehicle was free of the mud which had now been transferred to the Corporal. To make matters worse, once the Corporal had pushed the vehicle free of the mud, the Officer drove off and left him behind. It was a cold night; the Corporal was wet, covered in mud and a long way from anywhere. As the Police Vehicle was driven back along the airstrip, large chunks of mud were deposited all over the runway. The mud proved to be a hazard for Aircraft landing and taking off during the night flying exercise. The strip had to be cleaned before any further night flying could take place.

Once the Corporal had cleaned up, as best he could, we set about finding our Service Police vehicle, which was still missing. About twenty minutes later we found the vehicle parked outside the Officers Living-in Quarters. Our offender no doubt neatly tucked up in his warm bed. It took all my strength to stop my offsider from going in and strangling him as he slept. I should imagine the Officer had some explaining to do to the CO/OC the following day.

It was another cold night; I was on mobile patrol within the Base. Extra foot and mobile patrols were out as someone had broken into one of our Ammunition Depots and stolen some high explosives. We thought at the time it may have been Terrorists but we were to learn that it was an inside job, involving some of our Apprentices, living on the base. We had called in Investigators from our local 'Detachment B' along with Police dog handlers, to assist with the investigation and added security.

I was sitting beside another Service Policeman who was driving. We were in a Kombi Van; however this vehicle was from the base car pool and was not a Police vehicle. Our original Police vehicle was being used by some of the more senior members of our Branch who were assisting with the Investigation into the missing explosives. The vehicle we were in had no blue light, Police radio or fitted with a metal cage. We were using hand held radios to keep in contact with the Guard Room. As we drove through the night we observed vehicle lights in the distance, the lights were over to our right and on the Golf Course. We knew that the golf course was out of bounds to the use of vehicles. It appeared that someone was doing wheelies on the golf course as the vehicle was being driven erratically. As the Corporal and I were about to make our way towards this vehicle, the vehicle drove towards us, at great speed. We watched in amazement as the vehicle then disappeared into a large pile of sand that was being stored at the side of the golf course. We could then hear the motor of the vehicle revving at high pitch as the vehicle was reversed out of the pile of sand. The vehicle was then driven straight at us, cutting across our path. Once we saw the private vehicle we knew the owner/driver and once again knew we were about to be outranked.

The vehicle was stopped directly in front of our path, crossways and following the camber of the road. As the driver was about to step out of the vehicle, he obviously forgot to put the hand brake on and left the vehicle in gear as it rolled forward and went down a ditch, into the creek. The driver going along with his vehicle. As we moved our vehicle forward in line with the vehicle now in the creek we could just make out the red tail lamps. 'Do you think he can swim?' asked the Corporal. 'I hope so' I said 'As it is too bloody cold out there to go swimming.' We could see movement from the vehicle and then a soggy individual crawl up the embankment towards our vehicle. 'Quick lock all the doors, he is not getting into this warm vehicle in that state.' I said. As this soggy individual slid up the passenger side door of my vehicle, I heard 'Who are you?' 'Who the bloody hell are you' I said, knowing full well who I was speaking to.   After identifying myself I was told 'Put on your blue light' 'Sir, we don't have a blue light' 'Put on your blue light' I used the hand held radio in the vehicle to contact the Flight Sergeant in charge of my shift. I explained to the Flight Sergeant that if he did not come and rescue me from this soggy individual he might have a drowning investigation on his hands.

Another incident involving the same Officer comes to mind. I was on night shift on the base and it was about 0300 hours (3am) when the Officer decided that he was going to police, speeding on the base. At 3am you would have to be joking, anyone with an ounce of sense would be in bed asleep. Not boy blunder. Our hero decided to chase another vehicle by using his private vehicle. (I must have hid the Police vehicle) He stated that the vehicle he was chasing was speeding on the base; this was after he ran into the back of the alleged speedster. Apparently one of the base cooks was reporting for duty in his private vehicle when he slowed down on the base to make a right hand turn into one of the car parks. The next thing he knew was that a vehicle had come out of nowhere and ran into the back of his vehicle, scaring the hell out of him. I had enough work to do on my shift without a Traffic Accident Investigation. On arrival at the crash scene I took one look at the length of the skid marks on the road left by the Officers private vehicle and decided to buy out of the investigation, leaving it for a more Senior Investigator. Explain that traffic accident to your insurance company.

My last memory of this Officer was when he was in charge of an Honour Guard at the main gate. The Honour Guard was to salute the arrival of the Governor General (Kerr) who was to attend the base. Unfortunately the Governor Generals entourage was not only late in arriving but entered the base through the outgoing entrance. As the Honour Guard were all facing forward at the incoming entrance of the gate, the whole Honour Guard had to be about turned to greet the Governor General coming through the wrong gate. By the time the Governor General arrived it was almost dark and all we saw of him was his silver hair. As the Guard was about turned to greet the GG, the Officer, having his sword in his hand, swung madly around and caught the end of the sword, in the cape, worn by the Padre. On the original Honour Guard the Base Padre was standing at the rear of the guard and at the rear of the Officer in charge of the guard.

On the about turn the Padre was now standing in front of the entire guard with the Officer behind him waving madly with his sword. The sword had got caught up in the rear ties of the Padre's black cape, which he had on over his RAAF uniform. The sword, being sharp, cut through the ties of the cape causing it to fall to the feet of the Padre as the GG drove by. It was the funniest event that I had seen in years. I don't think the GG would have noticed as it was so bloody dark the Honour Guard was a waste of time. I did not stay around to hear the discussion between the two Officers as they would probably not have appreciated my laughter. Every time that I see a sword being used in a general salute I cannot help smile to myself.

RAAF SCHOOL OF RADIO – RAAF BASE LAVERTON

Apprentices from the RAAF School of Radio were stationed at RAAF Base, Laverton when I was there. The majority of these apprentices were well behaved and caused very little trouble on the Base. Occasionally, just occasionally the Service Police were called to investigate the odd incident.

The RAAF had a responsibility as to the welfare of the Apprentices like all its service personnel. The Apprentices more so, as most of them were not old enough to drink or drive. The Apprentices lived in on the Base and were subject to a lot more restrictions than the average Airman. When they weren't studying or training, some would no doubt, get into mischief.

One of the investigations that I was involved in concerning some of the Apprentices was at the request of Telecom. I was asked to investigate how a Red Pay Telephone, situated in the foyer of the Apprentices living – in quarters, could be used to make several hundred dollars' worth of calls and yet contain no money. Easy ask one of the Apprentices. On a previous investigation involving vandalism of this Telephone, by the use of super glue, we overcame the problem by threatening to remove the Telephone from the foyer. We now had a new problem, still no money in the Telephone, however no damage. The little buggers were trying to outsmart us once again. This time the investigation revealed that the Apprentices were putting money in the phone to make their call however once the call was completed, they would unscrew the Telephone from the shelf in the foyer, tip the phone upside down and retrieve their money. The telephone would then be screwed back onto the shelf as if nothing had been tampered with. We overcame this problem by having the nut and bolt, holding the Telephone to the shelf, welded together so that the Telephone could not be unscrewed from the shelf. I think after that they were into short circuiting or something like that. After all, these kids were being taught in communications so I guess the Telephone was used as another training aid. I know that by the time I left RAAF Base Laverton I could just about make any call from a public telephone without dropping in a cent.

Some of the Apprentices had driver's licences as well as a motor vehicle parked on the Base. The occasional burnout took place and owning an unregistered or unroadworthy vehicle were all part of growing up. These problems were never major as an Apprentice could not afford to be removed from course.

Finally one further investigation that I remember involving some of the Apprentices, did not start out with them in mind, it started with a deficiency of beer in the Officers Mess. I was required to investigate a deficiency behind the bar in the Officers Mess and to cut a long story short, the investigation revealed that several kegs of beer had been emptied, over a period of time, without any financial reward. I cleared the bar staff however we could not account for several full kegs being emptied or the full kegs ever having been behind the bar. It was a mystery, as full kegs were counted when they came in, the empties were counted in storage and everything tallied, however we were still missing the odd full keg of beer. The theft of the beer had to be someone on the base who knew where the beer was stored and where the empty kegs were kept. It was during the investigation that one of the cooks from the Officers Mess informed me that he had seen Apprentices hanging around the Officers Mess very late at night or very early in the mornings. I could not understand why any Apprentice would need to be anywhere near the Officers Mess, day or night.

The investigation concerning the missing contents of several kegs then moved to the School of Radio, Apprentice lines. General enquiries carried out amongst the Apprentices revealed that several members had access to alcohol, each night, after their dry canteen had closed. This information had to be thoroughly investigated as the Apprentices were not allowed access to alcohol at any time during their training as most were under age. The only drinks that were allowed to be sold and purchased in the Apprentice's canteen were soft drinks, flavoured milk or water. The Apprentice's canteen, like the Airmen's canteen was a place of rest and relaxation after work. The only difference being Alcohol was not available in the Apprentice's canteen, so we thought.

Having their own Orderly Officers and Senior Apprentice's it was difficult to imagine how a group of Apprentice's could consume alcohol in their canteen, after hours and not get caught, let alone keep it a secret for so long. I believe a lot more Apprentices were involved than the investigation revealed. Senior members had to be in the know, had to be involved and no doubt look outs were required as the canteen could be inspected at any time. The object of the investigation was to find out where the alcohol was coming from and the main people involved. A thorough search of the building used by the Apprentice's as their canteen revealed an elaborate "beer on tap" setup in the ceiling. A manhole in the ceiling, directly above the service counter of the canteen, was used to lower lines, fitted with a tap, to pour beer. Two 9 gallon kegs were found in the ceiling along with all the implements to tap the kegs. Along with the two kegs were two deck chairs and several Co2 fire extinguishers. It would appear that once the kegs were tapped and the lines fed down to the counter in the canteen, two Apprentices would sit in the deck chairs and freeze the outside of the tapped kegs with the fire extinguishers. Cold beer on tap. I told you that they were clever little buggers. How many kegs or fire extinguishers these Apprentices had used was anyone's guess. The investigation revealed that the two kegs in the ceiling had been stolen from the Officer's Mess on the base and replaced with empty ones, hoping that the original full kegs would go unnoticed. Several Apprentices' involved in the initial theft were no doubt punished but as it was not the crime of the century, I do not remember any member being removed from course.

    I would not like to be accused of selective sections in this book which would paint a picture of me as a perfect policeman, as I was not. I had my faults like everyone else. I was charged for assault while serving at RAAF Base Laverton. Something I am not proud of, a spur of the moment incident on my part and I was subsequently charged by the RAAF for my actions.

    I was conducting an interview with an Airman, who had been accused of hitting his mate on the head with a crash helmet. I left the interview room to get something from my desk which was just outside the room. I had left my desk neat, tidy and free of clutter when I went into the interview room. My desk was now covered in paper, a typewriter sitting on the top, my desk drawer open and containing food scraps. I asked the CPL Service Policeman present, as to why he left my desk in such a state while his desk, which was a few feet away, was not used. I obviously did not like his reply as I told him that if he made a mess on my desk again, I would cuff him one in the ear. I think I got another smart remark so I flicked the member on the right ear with my open hand. I regretted the incident immediately as it was a knee jerk reaction. The CPL ran straight to the FSGT in charge of the section and informed him that I had struck him in the ear. The CPL was entitled to report the matter as I should not have cuffed him. The FSGT came out of his office and asked me if I had struck the CPL, I said 'yes' and he suspended me of all duties, on the spot. I was suspended from duties for two weeks, I had to report for work every day, sit behind my desk and do nothing, not even answer a phone. At the end of the two weeks, the local Service Police Detachment sent out two of its members to interview me over the assault. It would have been one of the easiest Records of Interview that they had ever done as I helped them draft it as the interview progressed. About a week later a report from the Detachment was sent to the Commanding Officer, Base Squadron, RAAF Base Laverton, recommending that I be charged for assaulting another Service Policeman.

The day finally came when I had to front the CO for striking another RAAF member. I received a reprimand and told to march out of the room. A few minutes later I was called back into the CO's office along with the CPL that I had struck. I was stunned when the CO berated the CPL, in front of me, for leaving half eaten food in my desk drawer. I was then asked by the CO if I could still work with the CPL. The CPL was asked by the CO if he could still work with me. I informed the CO that I would have no trouble in working with the CPL and, without thinking, added, as long as he does not leave my desk in a mess as I will hang one on him. The last words that I remember the CO saying to me were 'Get Out' 'Get Out' As they say in the movies, I decamped the area, quick smart.

About two weeks later I was informed that I had been posted to No1 Stores Depot, RAAF Tottenham, about 30 minutes further up the road. I was not sure if I was due for posting or I had hurried it along a bit. I did not mind the posting as I did not have to uproot my family from the local caravan park. All I required from the base was my posting orders and my pay book. I would miss the friends that I had made while serving at Laverton, however life goes on and I would eventually catch up with most of my friends again.

I do not believe that there were any hard feelings on behalf of the CPL, that I struck, and myself, as we were on a training course together a couple of times after the incident. I certainly held no grudge. Being charged for assault was a wakeup call for me as the remainder of my RAAF service was without further legal action.

During my posting at RAAF Base Laverton I carried out almost every type of Police investigation, except murder. As previously stated, I do not intend to discuss, in detail, any serious investigations that I was involved in during my RAAF career but I will mention that I was attacked with a knife during my time on the base. The "Bacardi Kid" will remember the incident along with the little shit responsible. I will also mention that on attending a Domestic, off of the base, I was confronted by an Airman holding a fully loaded .22 rifle. It was certainly an interesting two and a half years that I spent on the base. I enjoyed my time there and my best memories are of the Service Police members who I served with and the stories I have mentioned. Now on to my next posting, No 1 Stores Depot, RAAF Tottenham, Victoria; about 30 minutes' drive from Laverton.

_____

The Author – A122073 Corporal Tony Wayne Maurice Easterby – RAAF Police Badge Number 241

RAAF Base Laverton, Victoria 1973-74. Author on left, CPL B. Spillane on right. Tarmac Jackets worn for cold winter nights.

RAAF Base Laverton, Victoria 1973-74. CPL T. Dimond on left, Author on right, note the SP armbands and also the white caps. We had the white caps for a trial period and went from being called "Screws" to "Snowdroppers."

CHAPTER 29

N01 STORES DEPOT – RAAF Tottenham

My arrival at No 1 Stores Depot, RAAF Tottenham, took place in September 1974, and I was given a married quarter on the base which allowed me to walk to work each day, the only down side being, that I was on call 24 hours a day, 7 days a week. I spent four years on this Depot during which I was to work with some exceptional Service Policemen. I will not use their real names only their nick names, "Squirty W", "Rodney Rocket", and "Mr. Asia". These members taught me a lot about Police work. I was promoted to Sergeant during my posting and it was also during this posting that I was to become a member of a murder investigation team. The murder did not take place on the base however involved the RAAF. Unfortunately this murder has never been resolved and as I write, I have again asked the Victoria Police to re-open the investigation as a cold case.

I was no doubt involved in several funny incidents on the Depot during my time there; unfortunately I can only remember one. It all started one afternoon when the Sergeant in charge of the Service Police decided that we needed to do a "Stake Out" on an Airman who was believed to be sneaking ladies into his single living in quarters. As the male, single living in quarters, were out of bounds to females, it was therefore an offence by the Airman to invite ladies to his room. I was informed by the Sergeant that he and I would be involved in the investigation and that I was to report for duty, late that night, to carry out surveillance of the Airmen's room. I was to wear dark clothing. About 2300 hours (11pm) we took up a position in the bushes outside the Airmen's quarters, near where we could observe the ground floor window of his room. It was suspected that he was asking his lady friends to climb through this window to enter his room. (Why I do not know as the block had a perfectly good front door) We had blackened our faces and had also put on dark beanies. (We definitely watched too many movies) We lay on our stomachs within the bushes, outside the quarters and it would have been easy to go to sleep, but being Victoria and bloody cold, there was not much chance of that. It was about 0200 hours (2am) and I don't even think the Airman was in his quarters, when this lone figure walked towards our position in the bushes. The Sergeant nudged me to ensure that I was awake. The figure came closer and closer until it stood directly in front of our position, as if knowing that we were there. Being good surveillance officers that we were, we remained perfectly still, not giving our positions away. Imagine our surprise when this lone figure urinated into the bushes on top of us. It turned out that the offending piddler was a drunk and on his way home from a night out on the town. Of all the places that he needed to take a piddle. We stood our ground as we could imagine the story around the Depot, next day, "Drunk pees on Service Police hiding in bushes" We left the area a short time later. My wife asking as to why I was showering so early in the morning.

The Depot was the first time, in my RAAF career, that I had a falling out with an Officer. To me it was always a matter of Principle. I will let you decide who was right or wrong.

It all started when I was ordered to remove my military campaign ribbons from my RAAF blue shirt. When I asked as to why I had to remove my ribbons, I was informed that it was a RAAF Policy requirement, as the blue shirts were too thin to have anything pinned to them. The only place campaign ribbons were to be worn was on the RAAF uniform jacket. I said that I did not have a problem if that was the Policy however I wanted to know as to why the RAAF allowed their Officers to wear their metal brevets on their shirts as they were a lot heavier than my ribbons. I was never given a satisfactory answer at any time however I had to remove my campaign ribbons from my shirt. To cut a long story short I went through correct military channels in pointing out what seemed to be one rule for Officers and another for Airmen when it came to wearing ornaments on the RAAF uniform shirt.

Each time I was told not to make waves and refused each time to return my campaign ribbons to my shirt.

After having exhausted all avenues of approach concerning the wearing of my campaign ribbons, I decided to write to the then Minister for Defence, the Hon (James) D.J. Killen. I advised the Minister of my concern about not being permitted to wear my military campaign ribbons on an approved military uniform. I also mentioned the fact that there appeared to be one rule for RAAF Officers and a separate rule for Airmen when it came to the so called Policy, regarding wearing of ornaments on the RAAF uniform shirt. I also pointed out to the Minister that if I was a bus driver or a scout master or anyone else wearing an approved uniform, I would have an automatic right to wear my military campaign ribbons on that uniform.

The Minister agreed with me and in his forwarding correspondence, he advised me to return my campaign ribbons to my RAAF uniform shirt and that he would have the RAAF Policy changed.

When I presented a copy of the Ministers letter to the Officer concerned and the Depot Orderly room, all hell broke loose and I was accused of being a trouble maker and going over everyone's head. I was in the bad books for several weeks (what was new), however about a week later every Airman or Airwoman, entitled to campaign ribbons, could wear them proudly on their approved RAAF uniform, including their shirts. To me it was a matter of Principle to pursue the matter as I believed the RAAF was wrong in what they were doing. One rule for all, not segregation.

I will mention a rather ugly incident that I was involved in at a time when I was in charge of the Police Section on the Depot. I had been ordered by a RAAF Officer to attend a RAAF married quarter, off base, and return with an Airman who was not only AWOL but was refusing to return to the Depot after having been ordered to by the Officer.

I had dealt with this Airman before as he was the little shit who had stuck a loaded .22 rifle in my face about two years before when I was serving at RAAF Base Laverton. I had attended a domestic between the Airman and his wife, at the request of his wife; however when I tried to calm everyone down, the Airman decided to get his .22 Rifle and threaten everyone.

This time it was not much different, the Airman and his wife were again both in a state of high aggression. The Airman was refusing to return to the Depot with me as he and his wife wanted him out of the RAAF. When I informed the Airman that I was not leaving without him and that I would place him under arrest, he opened a side cupboard and pulled out a double barrel shotgun and aimed it at me, saying that he was not going anywhere. His wife then became hysterical which made matters worse.

I should have walked away and returned with the civil police; unfortunately for both of them they caught me on a bad day. I was not only pissed off with having a shotgun stuck in my face, but I had been informed about two days earlier, by my then wife, that after 13 years of marriage she was leaving me for another man. I was therefore not in a good state of mind and by rights should not have been on the job.

All the police training, involving the situation that I now faced, went out the window. Common sense should have told me to walk away and get the civil police. I was now angry as this little shit had pulled a weapon on me before and the RAAF let him off with a warning not to do anything like that again. I was not going to allow it to happen a second time and he would get his wish to leave the RAAF, providing he did not kill me in the meantime. I gave the Airman the options of, using the weapon or if I decided to take it off of him that I was going to beat him to a pulp or he could put down the weapon, return with me to the Depot and that I would guarantee his removal from the RAAF.

The Airman chose to return to the Depot with me and when he put the weapon down; he could not understand why I handcuffed his hands behind his back to return him to his Unit. When I checked the Shotgun I found it to be unloaded, as apparently his wife hid any ammunition that she found in the house, but she was not sure if he had found some to load the shotgun. She, like me thought the shotgun was loaded

The Airmen's wife, who was still yelling and screaming at both of us, wanted to accompany her husband back to the Depot and confront his boss. I politely informed her that she was not travelling in my RAAF vehicle and if she insisted that I would lock her in the boot. I had had a gut full of both the Airman and his wife.

When I returned the Airman to the Officer concerned, the Officer could not understand why I had returned his Airman in handcuffs. I was in no mood for the poor Airman bit and as I was about to get everything off of my chest, in through the door burst the Airmen's wife. Once I had uncuffed the Airman, all hell broke loose, the last I saw of the Officer, the Airman and the Airmen's wife; they were all chasing each other around the room. I immediately left the building, made my way to the Depot gymnasium and took my frustrations out on the punching bag for the remainder of the afternoon.

The following day I made it quite clear to the Officer that he could recommend Discharge of the Airman concerned or we could consider a Court Marshall, it was up to him. The Airman received his discharge from the RAAF and I for one was not sorry to see him go.

Minus two, according to the weather bureau as I walked through the rear gate, of my on base married quarter to make my way to the RAAF Police office. It was 7.30 am, the frost on the base oval which I had to cross, was thick like snow and within a few minutes my leather shoes were wet through. God I hated the cold in Victoria. I had not been in the Police Office long trying to get warm and dry my shoes, when the telephone rang. It was one of the Depot RAAF Officers stating that the driver of a delivery truck, attending the store, was acting weird and may be under the influence of drugs.

On attending the warehouse I was directed towards a young lad sitting in the Officers office drinking a coffee. On looking at the lad and noticing how young he appeared and how small he was, I could not imagine him being the driver of the large Semi Trailer parked in the store. The lad would have been 16-17 years of age and if he could see over the dashboard of the truck it would have been a miracle. As I was about to establish the identity of the lad the driver of the Semi-Trailer appeared from the Toilet area of the Warehouse. The driver stated that the lad was not his offsider or that he knew who the lad was, he certainly did not bring him to the Depot.

After a thorough investigation it was established that the lad was mentally impaired and that he had wandered away from a disabled group dance party, the night before. The dance hall was several miles from the RAAF Depot and the lad had been wandering about all night with very little warm clothes or with anything to eat or drink. It was further established that the lad had walked alongside the Semi-Trailer, when it entered the Depot. The lad was on the opposite side of the vehicle as it passed through the Security Guard gate; therefore he was not seen by the guard on duty. When the local Civil Police were contacted they informed me that they had been looking for the lad since he had wandered away from the dance the night before.

It was so obvious that this lad could not have been the driver of the Semi-Trailer parked on the Depot and that he was mentally impaired when spoken to. Sometimes you had to wonder about our future leaders of tomorrow.

No 1 Stores Depot, when I was there, was used, for a short time, as a basic training unit for the intake of WRAAF's. Our RAAF Police unit at the Depot provided the lectures on Drug Education. It was also the first and only Unit that I was required to lock up an Airwoman in the Depot Cells, at the main gate guard room. The ACW was locked in the cells at the request of her Commanding Officer. I mention this because it was very unusual to lock up a female in unit guard room cells.

The posting to No1 Stores Depot had a great effect on my life as well as my RAAF career as it was during this time that my first marriage ended. I had by then, three lovely children who, along with their mother, moved interstate. This left a very big hole in my life, from which I have never really recovered. Not growing up with your children leaves you very empty inside.

During my posting at No1 Stores Depot, in 1975, the Police Mustering changed its name from "Service Police" to "RAAF Police" and our armbands were replaced with a metal RAAF Police badge, secured to a leather tag, which was then hung from the top button, above the left breast, of your uniform. My badge number was 241. Non Commissioned RAAF Police received silver badges while the Provost Officers received gold badges. These badges would normally remain with you during your entire career and you were given the opportunity to retain the badge on discharge from the RAAF

It would be remiss of me if I did not mention the RAAF Police Dog Handlers at No1 Stores Depot, RAAF Tottenham, as without their help and dedication to the job at hand, my work at the Depot would have been a lot harder. The love and training that these members give to their dogs is beyond belief. I have the utmost respect for the Police Dog Mustering and had the pleasure of working with them on many occasion.

RAAF Police No 9 Drug Investigation Course – Headquarters RAAF Provost Unit – 1977. Author front row, third from right.

CHAPTER 30
RAAF BASE POINT COOK – VICTORIA

In June 1978 I was posted to RAAF Base Point Cook, I was now divorced and living alone in a 25 foot mobile home which I had purchased. It was during the time that I was living alone that I completed the draft of my first book, GREEN MULES GREEN GIANTS. On completion of the draft it sat in a drawer until 2002, partly because the section on Borneo Operations was Top Secret until 1996.

I did not like the idea of living in a single man's quarters on a RAAF Base so that was why I purchased a mobile home; I could tow the big van to where ever my next posting would be. This plan fell to pieces however when I met the most wonderful woman a man could ever wish for. This lady had two lovely boys of her own from her first marriage and when I could bring my children across from interstate, they all enjoyed each other's company. I eventually asked that lovely lady to marry me and we are still as happy today as when we first met.

It had been six years since I completed my basic Police Training at Point Cook and now I had been given the opportunity to take up a new posting as the Sergeant in charge of the RAAF Police, on the Base.

As I entered the Base on my first day, the Guard on the Main Gate waved me through without, not only checking my identity, but not even taking his feet off of the little desk in front of him. I was not impressed. Point Cook was the home of the Air Force and as I was to be responsible for the Base Security I was about to make a few changes.

I stopped at the Guard Gate, made the young Airman stand to attention and asked him if he had been instructed to check the identity of everyone entering the Base. He advised me that his orders were to identify everyone entering the base but thought it okay to wave through anyone wearing a RAAF uniform. I quietly advised the Airman that I was the new Sergeant in charge of the RAAF Police on the unit and as of that moment he would check the identification of everyone entering the base and those people not in possession of a RAAF Identity card would be required to report to the Guard Commander for a pass to enter the base. No exceptions and I would brief the Guard Commander. After briefing the Guard Commander and meeting up with some of the RAAF police who would be working for me, I proceeded to the Base Squadron Orderly Room where I was to meet my new boss, the Commanding Officer, Base Squadron, RAAF Base Point Cook.

My new boss was an ex-navigator who flew in a F111, one hell of a nice guy. When I advised the CO about the security incident at the Main Gate, he leaped across his desk and I thought he was going to flatten me, instead he shook my hand, saying it was about time that he had a Police Officer who was interested in the job. I was stunned as I had no knowledge of any problems with the RAAF Police on the base. I was not to find many problems really; all that was needed was a firm directive as to why RAAF Police were required on the base, what our responsibilities were and what was expected of the 10 RAAF Police under my charge. My main instruction to the eight men, two women, was that, if they had made a mistake, at any time, while carrying out their duties that I was to be the first person notified. I was not to hear of their mistakes from anyone else. That was my only specific order and it worked quite well. This order gave me time to assess any problems that might arise as my first priority was the welfare of my troops. This rule served me well in the Army and it would serve me well in the RAAF. From day one I had a good working relationship with my CO and OC of the base along with the 10 Corporal RAAF Police.

Point Cook was one of the happiest postings of my RAAF career,

I applied for a married quarter on the base, and Joy and I were married in the little chapel on the base and by the base Padre. The RAAF police gave us a guard of honour on our wedding day, one member was my best man while another was the wedding photographer. The Sergeant's Mess held our wedding reception while one of the Base cooks made our beautiful wedding cake. We had approximately fifty guests at our reception including my three children, my wife's two children, her parents and three of my sisters/ sister –in-law. It was a great time in my life.

Now back to the running of the Police Section on the base. The first week that I spent at Point Cook in the capacity of the Sergeant in charge of Police, I put on a 9 gallon keg at the Airmen's Canteen so that I could introduce myself to one and all. This worked quite well and it did not take me long to identify some of the members who I believed that I would have to keep an eye on. Point Cook, at that time, like RAAF Laverton, was an operational base. We had a large Flight Training School where future RAAF pilots learnt to fly for the first time. We had an Officer Training School on the base along with a large Maintenance Depot and Transport Depot. Also with Aircraft, a large Fire Section manned 24 hours a day by RAAF Firemen. Along with all these Units we had a group who owned, restored and flew Vintage Aircraft. Surprisingly however not a big base for crime, we had our serious offences and investigations but overall not a bad base to work on. The biggest offenders of small crimes like graffiti, vandalism and the odd break/enter were some of the kids living with their RAAF parents, on the base. Even though the Base provided them with their own hobby hut, pool room etc they still managed to cause problems around the area. You had to watch where you parked the RAAF Police Van when you patrolled the base at night as the little buggers would put glass bottles under the wheels of the van and steal the RAAF Police magnetic signs.

Not to mention the time that they broke into the Base Gun Club and emptied the biggest bottle of Scotch whisky, you have ever seen, onto the floor. If you are a whisky lover you would have cried at the useless waste.

Point Cook was a very difficult base to secure as the entire perimeter had nothing other than a few strands of barbed wire fence, a Main Gate and large open beach area facing Port Phillip Bay. Surprisingly, because the whole base was patrolled day and night, by the RAAF Police, very few breaches of security were encountered. Even when the local RAAF Police Detachment (Detachment B) decided to carry out a mock Security Penetration exercise, we faired pretty well and picked up most of their members who had entered the base illegally. It was also not unusual to assist the local civil Police in locating bodies that would wash up on the beach adjoining the base. It would appear that if someone drowned in the bay, and the body was not located within a short time, it would generally wash up on the beach at Point Cook, something to do with the tide.

I remember one such incident when we were asked to look out for a body of a person who had jumped off of the pier in Williamstown. I had asked to borrow a four wheel drive from the base Transport section, to drive along the beach adjoining the base as our Police vehicle, a Kombi, was not designed for driving through sand. The four wheel drive that we were given had a canvas covered back, so to stand a few Police members in the back, to look out along the beach, as we patrolled, we removed the canvas. This then left a steel frame at the back of the vehicle for members to hang onto. When we started the patrol along the beach we had a full metal frame, however when I got to the end of the beach I got out to talk to the members standing in the back, I noticed that the steel frame was missing. The steel frame was made up of several sections and as each section fell off onto the beach, the members in the back just moved onto the next section until it to disappeared. They were that engrossed in trying to locate the body that they did not notice the steel frame on the vehicle had disappeared. This had to be some sort of omen, for as we moved back along the beach with two policemen walking in front of the vehicle, picking up the metal pieces, we found the body. The body had only been reported missing a few days however it was buried flush with the sand on the beach, we had almost driven over it. The body was that of a small frail female and could not be seen from the vehicle as we patrolled. Another time we borrowed a four wheel drive to search along the beach and as we had to cross an area of sand where the tide was now coming in I asked one of my illustrious members to check the depth of the water before we drove across. His idea of checking the depth of the water consisted of throwing a piece of stick in it, which was quickly swept away.

'Yeah it's okay to cross boss' came the reply. As the driver of the vehicle attempted the crossing, the front of the vehicle disappeared to the windscreen, we had driven into quicksand. We were sinking and looked like losing a RAAF vehicle, for which I was responsible. You will not live that one down "Gunnar"

Thank god for the Base Fire Section who came to our rescue and managed to save the vehicle from completely being submerged. It was close and I had some explaining to do to the CO, next day.

It was during my time at Point Cook that my CO encouraged me to apply for a Commission within the RAAF. The only problem being that the only Commission that I would have been interested in was within my own Mustering and that being a Provost Officer. Two things prevented me from even considering a Commission and that was, I did not have the education required or the experience in the Mustering. I had attained my Junior Level of education in the Army but nothing further, it was time for me to go back to school.

I must admit, the RAAF encourages its members to further their education, as I was informed that if I was prepared to go back to school and pass my exams, the RAAF would pay the bill. I then set about attending Footscray TAFE College, two nights a week, for a year. Within the first year I attained my Leaving Certificate. As I required Tertiary subjects to be considered for a Commission, I again signed up at TAFE for a further two years, to complete my Certificate in Police Studies. Fortunately after turning in my first assignment on Communication and Report writing, I was told that the Course would be of no value to me as I was well ahead of the standard that they required, I was given a Credit for the year and told to nick off. I was to then sign up for the following subjects Forensic Science and Behavioral Studies. Unfortunately a week into the course I was posted into the city, however I managed to complete the course even while working shift work, thanks to an understanding Provost Officer. The reason for my posting to the Detachment was that on applying for a Commission, the OC of the Base requested that I spend some time in the Detachment to help further my application. The Detachment would not accept me on temporary attachment therefore I was posted, much to my disappointment. I had to leave my married quarter on the Base and move into another married quarter in Werribee.

My wife and I were in our Werribee married quarter less than 12 months before I was posted again.

One of the most unusual investigations that I was involved in during my RAAF career took place at Point Cook. I was required to carry out an investigation at the Base Fire Section hangar where a Dragster motor vehicle, had driven into one of the hangar doors, causing the hangar door to be knocked from its rollers. The door subsequently falling to the ground on top of the Dragster. When you think of the size of an Aircraft hangar and the size of one of the two hangar doors, it is hard to imagine a door being knocked off its rollers.

When I attended the scene I found a Dragster motor vehicle underneath the hangar door. The door being made up of heavy steel frames and covered with corrugated iron, weighed several tons. Fortunately when the hangar door fell on top of the Dragster, the corrugated iron was the only material to make contact with the vehicle. A steel roll over bar, fitted above the driver's seat, of the Dragster, took the impact. The corrugated iron tearing apart, all around the drivers cabin of the Dragster. I was not to know at that time that someone had been driving the Dragster and had been sitting in the driver's seat when the hangar door fell on him. To cut a long story short I was told initially that the owner of the Dragster was working outside the vehicle, revving the motor, when the vehicle suddenly took off and ran into the closed hangar door. The story appeared to have a few holes in it as far as I was concerned.

The owner of the Dragster, who was a RAAF Fireman, had been given permission, by his boss, to carry out some mechanical work on the Dragster while he was at work. No permission had been given for the Dragster to be driven in the hangar or around the base.

On inspecting the concrete floor of the hangar I noted several, long black skid marks. These skid marks were of the same width, of the two large black slick tyres, that were on the rear of the Dragster. When the truth finally came out, the owner of the vehicle had been taking the Dragster for short runs within the hanger when he lost control, due to the enormous power, of the vehicle. The vehicle had got away from him on one of the runs and he could not stop it in time before running into one of the closed hangar doors. He received only a minor cut and some bruises. Had one of the steel door frames fallen on him, he would no doubt have been killed.

To complete my story at RAAF Base Point Cook, I served with some exceptional RAAF Police on the base and again it would be remiss of me if I did not mention two incidents which indicated just how dedicated some members were to the job. On one occasion a RAAF Police member was called to attend a possible suicide where a member had gassed himself in his motor vehicle. The Policeman, on attending the scene, broke into the vehicle, pulled the victim out, cleared his airway and proceeded to give him mouth to mouth resuscitation. Unfortunately the member was already deceased. If you have any idea as to what happens to people who gas themselves in a motor vehicle you would understand just how difficult it would be to consider giving that person mouth to mouth. That Corporal is a man among men in my book. A further incident involving another Corporal RAAF Policeman was where a vintage Tiger Moth aircraft, crashed a few hundred meters from the Main Gate/Police Office. The aircraft burst into flames on hitting the ground and being made up of only wood/canvas burnt fiercely. This however did not stop the Policeman from attempting to brave the flames and to try and rescue the pilot. Unfortunately the ball of flame on impact burnt everything beyond recognition.

Times like these made me proud to be part of such a worthwhile organization.

In November 1978 I was attached to RAAF Base Fairbairn NSW to complete a Commonwealth Police Supervisors Course 2/78. The course was held at the Commonwealth Police Training establishment in the ACT. I attended the establishment, once again, several years later to complete a Federal Police Traffic Accident Course.

Sometime in 1979, I believe, the RAAF Police mustering was divided into two separate groups, one covering RAAF Police investigations and the other RAAF Police security. I remained an Investigator even though promotion was now a little faster if you decided to remuster to the Police security section.

RAAF Police No 22 Investigators Course – 1978. Headquarters RAAF Provost Unit, Melbourne Victoria – Author back row, first left.

RAAF Police No 22 Field Security Course – 20th July 1979 – Author middle row, first on right.

CHAPTER 31
DETACHMENT B – MELBOURNE

It was in January 1980 that I was posted to Detachment B, Gratton Street, Carlton, Melbourne, Victoria. By now I had just about moved into my married quarter in Werribee. I was employed on Criminal and Drug investigations within the Detachment and given a secondary job as manager of the Detachments (bulk) bar stock. The secondary job was to assist me with my application for a Commission, where I could demonstrate administration capabilities. I was also given permission to complete my night course at TAFE to secure my Certificate in Police Studies. Anytime that I was rostered on night duties during my TAFE course I could make up the time during the day. It worked out well and I completed my Tertiary Education. Part of working in the Drug Section was to attend local RAAF Units and run drug awareness lectures. It was at one of these lectures that an Officer ate my Marijuana plant. I had just completed a drug lecture to a new group of Trainee Officers, at Officer Training School, RAAF Base Point Cook. I had been given the Marijuana plant as a training aid from the Victoria Police Drug Investigation branch when another RAAF Policeman and I assisted them in a drug raid. The Marijuana plant was a great specimen, numerous green leaves and about a meter high. It was after I had completed the lecture when this Officer came up, stripped all the leaves from my plant and ate them. I was stunned, (I bet he was a short time later). When I asked him why he ate the leaves of my plant, he advised me he always wanted to see what Marijuana leaves tasted like. I should have locked him up for use of a prohibited drug. Leaders of tomorrow. After the destruction of my Training Aid I sent away for a plastic look alike. Eat that and tell me what it tastes like. The RAAF did not have a drug problem at the time I served; I have no idea as to what it would be like today. Marijuana was the main drug that we came across however occasionally we sprung the odd Airman trying LSD. The RAAF had a no tolerance policy when it came to drugs, anything other than one puff of a Marijuana cigarette; you were discharged from the RAAF. I agreed with this policy as I have very little time for drug users or dealers.

As most investigations carried out by the Detachment involved local RAAF units, I got to visit all the RAAF bases within Victoria, sometimes having to live in on the base to complete an investigation. I had been at the Detachment for about 12 months when the RAAF decided that it would close all of its Detachments and send the members back to RAAF Units throughout Australia. I was posted to RAAF Base, Edinburgh, South Australia.

RAAF Police members of Detachment 'B', Melbourne, Victoria 1980.

CHAPTER 32

RAAF BASE, EDINBURGH, SOUTH AUSTRALIA

This section on my posting to RAAF Base Edinburgh will be a short one as I have very few happy memories of this posting. It was the worst posting of my RAAF career and the most costly, promotion wise. I arrived at my posting in January 1980; the RAAF Police Section was fairly large and had a Provost Officer on the base. I was soon to learn that I was not part of the in crowd. I was a Senior Investigator however I was put on permanent shift work in a mobile patrol section. I spent the next 12 months rattling locks. Patrol members were not allowed to leave the unit on patrol and eventually allowed no longer than 30 minutes in the RAAF police section to have a coffee. The crunch came when we had to report to the Guard Room and sign the guard book at regular intervals. Talk about trust. I served with a great group of Corporals and Sergeants. It was the only time in my RAAF career that I was disgusted with my own mustering. My night shift finished at 8am in the morning however it was not unusual to have to wait around to 9am while the coffee was made and the crossword completed, before you could brief anyone on the previous night's occurrences. I could understand why people would cut out the crossword from the paper, put in extra black squares or half complete the answers.

One of my happiest moments at RAAF Base Edinburgh was when I met Her Majesty. The Queen.

I had finished a night shift, 2400 hours to 0800 hours (midnight to 8am), when I was informed that all RAAF Police members were required for base duty, that day, as Her Majesty, The Queen was arriving at RAAF Base Edinburgh. I had time to go home, have breakfast, shower and put on a clean uniform. I was also required to wear my campaign medals on my RAAF uniform jacket.

My job, on the arrival of Her Majesty, was to control the local press and cameramen. The press, along with their cameramen had been allocated a designated, enclosed area, just left of the red carpet, which had been laid out on the Tarmac. My job was to ensure that none of the press or cameramen moved outside of the fenced enclosure. It was probably one of the best positions of the entire event as The Queen and her party would walk right by us. Once The Queen and her entourage had passed us they would enter the building on the Tarmac where Her Majesty would be introduced to the waiting dignitaries

When the Royal Aircraft landed and Her Majesty walked along the red carpet, I saluted her as she drew level with my position. Instead of walking straight past me she stopped and quizzed me on my Borneo Campaign Medal, which she had spotted. She obviously recognized one of her own medal issues but was not aware of the two colour ribbons or medals, of the Vietnam campaign. In answer to her question about the Borneo Medal, I advised Her Majesty that I had served in Malaysia and Borneo from 1965 to 1967 with the Commonwealth Military Forces. I said that I was a 19 year old, Australian Infantry Soldier at the time. Her Majesty mentioned how pleased she was that Australia had assisted Britain and other forces in Malaysia at its time of need.

Not long after Her Majesty had entered the building on the Tarmac I was informed that I could stand down and go home. I had been on my feet for almost 16 hours. Time flies when you are having fun.

As I have trouble sleeping, sleep lightly and wake easily I would get very upset, when at least three days a week, two dear old ladies would wake me from my sleep just to talk to me and give me "The Awake" magazine. It did not matter how many times that I told them that I was a shift worker and please not to wake me, they would forget and rattle my door. So as not to race out and hit them with a big piece of four by four the next time they woke me, I decided to place a sign on the door of my married quarter. I called this sign The Shift Workers Prayer, it read something like this, "God is in his heaven, I, am in my bed, upset this combination, you wish you were dead. Before you touch my handle say a little prayer, because when I open this Bloody Door, you had better not be there" Amen. Funny I never had any further problems with people waking me up during the day.

The fact that I was marked down in my yearly assessment as a RAAF policeman while employed at RAAF Base Edinburgh during the year that I was there, would have had a serious affect on my chance of promotion. As far as my application for a Commission, I may as well have torn it up. The second happiest day that I can remember while serving on the base was when I was informed that I had been posted to Malaysia

CHAPTER 33
RAAF BASE BUTTERWORTH – MALAYSIA

December 1981 saw my wife and I arrive in Malaysia, this was to be one of the happiest posting of my RAAF career and one which my wife enjoyed very much. Our RAAF married quarter was on the Island of Penang; however RAAF Base Butterworth was situated on the Malay Peninsular. It had been 16 years since I had lived in Malaysia, then serving with the 4th Royal Australian Regiment as an Infantry Soldier. While serving with the Army I lived in Malacca, Malaysia.

MALAYSIA

The Federation of Malaysia comprises of Peninsular Malaysia and the States of Sabah, Sarawak and Island of Borneo. In 1966 as an Infantry Soldier I fought against the Indonesian Army who were attempting to invade Sarawak and Sabah from Indonesian Borneo.

Malaysia has a population around 26 million, made up of Malays, Chinese, Indians and other ethnic groups, Approximately 60 percent of the population being Malays. Malays are also known as "Bumiputeras" or "sons of the soil" The National Language is Bahasa Melayu (Malay) however English is widely spoken. Thank goodness as my Malay/Indonesian is fairly poor even after a language course. The Malaysian currency being the Ringgit, which at the writing of this book was still worth about three Malaysian Ringgit to the Australian Dollar.

PENANG

Penang lies off the north/western coast of Peninsular Malaysia comprising the Island of Penang and Province Wellesley. The Capital being Georgetown. Approximately one million people live on the island and it is commonly referred to as 'The Pearl of the Orient." To get from the Island to mainland Malaysia, when I was stationed there with the RAAF, you crossed over by vehicle ferry, which took about 20 minutes. As we were leaving in 1984, the foundations for the bridge from Butterworth to the Island were being laid. When my wife and I visited Penang again in 2005 the new bridge had been completed. It is one of the longest bridges that I have travelled across and took about 13 minutes by vehicle

Now that you are a little familiar with both Malaysia and Penang let me continue with the story involving my RAAF posting. My wife, Joy, had never travelled outside of Australia before let alone asked to live in a foreign country. So it was a great culture shock for her, especially when she was dumped in a married quarter, late at night, on the Island and me having to report for work, first up, the following morning. My wife however handled the situation tremendously.

On arrival in Malaysia several of the RAAF Police wives, who were already living there, would ban together and organize your married quarter, by having the beds made and a basic groceries pack laid out for you, in the kitchen.

If you had small children, cots would be organized and made up. When you arrived in Malaysia, late in the evening on a flight from Australia, the last thing you would want to do, was make up beds or to try and organize food, for the next morning. This system worked fairly well and I think a lot of families were very grateful, I know that my wife and I were

There were three Australian Air Force Squadrons stationed at RAAF Butterworth when I arrived in 1981. Approximately 40 RAAF Police were needed to help maintain harmony and security for the servicemen and their families. Within a year of my arrival, the Australian Government decided to officially withdraw its Squadrons from Malaysia and two Squadrons returned home to Australia, along with families and about 30% of the RAAF Police. Postings then became 6 month duration. By 1987 Australia had no RAAF families living in Malaysia as part of its contingent. A few RAAF Aircraft remain there, with some maintenance personnel. I now believe that a small section of men, supplied by the Australian Army, on a 6 month rotation basis, are responsible for Aircraft security.

Our married quarter on the Island of Penang was at 3J Medam Lembah Permai, Tanjong Bungah, Penang Malaysia. It was a two storey unit with marble floors down stairs and parquetry floors upstairs. The downstairs area contained a main lounge area, kitchen, shower/toilet area and an Amahs room (Servants room). Upstairs contained four bedrooms with an on suite shower/toilet to the main bedroom.

Each room was fitted with a ceiling fan, which ran 24 hours a day, when you were home, as the humidity in Malaysia was unbearable at times. My wife employed a Chinese Amah who became part of our family. Ah Fun, as she was known, was employed to wash, iron and keep the home tidy. We did not require her to cook or live in. Ah Fun was married and had a family, so we required her to return home to her family each night. We enjoyed having Ah Fun around and if we could have found room in our suite cases we would have returned to Australia with her. Within a few days on arrival in Penang the new RAAF families attended a security briefing, normally given by the RAAF Padre, in company with a member of the RAAF Police. When I took up the position of Sergeant in charge of the RAAF Police on the Island, it was my duty to brief the new RAAF families on home and personal security.

It is now the first morning of my arrival in Malaysia and a RAAF Police vehicle has just arrived at my married quarter. I have to drop the Corporal RAAF Policeman off at his married quarter on the Island and then proceed to the Ferry, cross over to the mainland and report for duty at RAAF Butterworth. I was given a stick map on how to get to the Ferry and if you have ever driven in Malaysia for the first time, you would know that it is not that easy. Not knowing where you are going and traffic everywhere. By the time I found the vehicle Ferry and made my way across to the mainland, found the Air Base, I was about an hour late. You do not arrive late for duty in the Service.

I managed to make my way to the Main Guard Gate, RAAF Base Butterworth. I stopped the RAAF Police vehicle (Ford Sedan) in the left hand lane, with the right indicator working and my right hand extended, indicating that I was turning right into the Air Base.

As I was about 90 degrees into my turn, I caught a glimpse of a black object out of the corner of my right eye and instinct made me pull my right hand back inside the vehicle. The next moment I had a big pile of black metal stuck to the front of my Police vehicle. I had a black front guard, two black doors and a rear back guard, all from the side of a Morris Minor 1000 sedan. What was left of the Morris then proceeded to jump a large monsoon drain, drive about 100 meters along the wrong side of the road, and then change over to the correct side of the road, where it stopped. Once I had recovered from the shock I got out of my vehicle and ran up to the Morris to see if the occupants were okay. I do not know who got the biggest shock, the two occupants of the Morris or me. The male driver of the vehicle was just sitting there behind the steering wheel, still steering and looking straight ahead. Had he not been moving I would have thought he was dead. The driver, Malay, was wearing his little white hat which indicated that he had visited Mecca. The passenger, Malay female, whom I presume was the driver's wife, also sat staring straight ahead. They appeared not to notice that their vehicle no longer contained a left hand side. They also appeared not to notice that I was speaking to them, and as they were not injured, I left them in their little fantasy world and returned to the RAAF vehicle. I then moved all the Morris parts from the bonnet, placed the items in a big heap on the side of the road and proceeded to work. First stop, Transport Section, to fill out a traffic accident report. My first day on the job, my first of 13 accidents to come. Welcome to Malaysia "Wheels," as I was to become known.

I averaged about one traffic accident a month, for the first 12 months, so I will get all my traffic accidents out of the way, or some of them, I can't remember them all. I was not a bad driver however I did not have the temperament for driving in Malaysia, not for the first 12 months anyway. I thought the Malays would drive normally, after all they were supposed to have the same road rules as England and Australia. How wrong I was. Let me explain the Malaysian Road Traffic Act as seen by a tourist.

1. You only overtake another vehicle when there is oncoming traffic.
2. You may overtake the vehicle in front of you on either side, left or right, whatever takes you're fancy. Remember however that whatever side you may choose. another clown is probably using the other side to overtake and there is a good chance that you will collide with him when pulling in front of the vehicle that you are overtaking. This is very common when riding your step through (motorbike).
3. Don't pull in front of another vehicle unless the space remaining is only half the size of your vehicle, this will spoil your fun.
4. If you are driving a truck or a bus, remember you can remain permanently on the wrong side of the road until a much bigger vehicle than yours is coming in the opposite direction.
5. The best time to overtake is when the vehicle in front of you decides to turn left or right, as this way you can be sure to collide directly in the centre of the vehicle. Less chance of hurting someone and we are not speeding are we?
6. Finally the only two words that you really need to know in the Malay language to pass your driver's test is "ikit kiru" (keep left) you have to be kidding and "behenti (stop), especially given the order by the local police or you may receive a vehicle full of hot lead from a sub-machine gun.

Now that you are full bottle on the road rules on how to drive in Malaysia I will tell you about how my wife and I went to sit for our driver's license. The first day that we arrived at the licensing centre in Penang, we stood in the long line like everyone else to await our turn to sit for our Malaysian Driver's License. The normal thing to do in queue's in Malaysia is to push and shove and while no one is watching, queue jump. It was not unusual while you were waiting in line to have a little head appear under your armpit as people edged their way along the line. Anyway after a few too many queue jumpers, lots of pushing and shoving, the big Indian guard near the counter, had had enough and let fly into the ceiling of the building with both barrels of his double barrel shotgun. After the bits of plaster had settled my wife and I looked around as we were the only ones left standing in what was at one time, a queue. We decided however that we would go back another day and sit for our test. The annoying part about going through all the trouble of sitting for our tests for our Malaysian Drivers license was that a week after we received our license, your local grocery boy could obtain the license for you as long as you held a current driver's license, from another country. I began to wonder if someone told the licensing department about "Wheels," for me to have had to sit for the oral test.

My wife drove the three years in Malaysia without a traffic accident which is a feat all by itself. She did however receive a parking ticket after our little Morris, which was sporting a big red kangaroo on the boot, was singled out from two big Mercedes committing the same parking offence. Not one to give up lightly where one thinks there is an injustice; she sat in the police station all day arguing her case until the parking ticket was eventually torn up. The only other time that she encountered a problem on the road was when she was stopped at the only set of traffic lights on the island. A small motor bike pulled up alongside of her and part of the bike handle bars protruded into the driver's side window of the Morris. The handbrake on the handlebar was almost in her right ear. So as not to drive off from the lights and catch the bike handlebars in the window of the Morris, she gave the handlebars a gentle push as she drove away. On looking back, in the rear vision mirror in the Morris, she was horrified to find that she had laid out about 20 motorcycles on the roadway, opposite the traffic lights. The motorcycle that she pushed fell onto a series of other riders and laid them out in a domino effect. And they say "Wheels" was dangerous. Another one of my traffic accidents involving a RAAF Police vehicle happened one morning when I was on mobile patrol and travelling along a straight stretch of road, on the Island, that we called the mad mile. I was driving the vehicle, not travelling very fast and talking to a Corporal RAAF Policeman beside me. All of a sudden, out of nowhere came a cream coloured Mercedes sedan and overtook me. Unfortunately as the vehicle pulled in front of me the rear of the Mercedes caught the driver's side front bumper of my patrol vehicle causing it to spin off of the road in a 360 degree circle, with the vehicle coming to a halt in a large sand area. I was not impressed. I managed to start the little 120Y Datsun Sedan (Police Vehicle) and the chase was on, we were in hot pursuit. As the speedo of our little vehicle was showing signs of failure we began to gain on the Mercedes. My offsider by this time was trying to tighten his seat belt and at the same time trying to crawl under the dashboard where he thought he would be safe. These young ones, no sense of adventure. I managed to gain on the Mercedes vehicle, pass it and in true Hollywood style, pull up across the road blocking the driver's path. Unfortunately for the driver of the Mercedes vehicle he forgot to lock his driver's door as I pulled him from the vehicle demanding to know why he had run me off of the road and keep going. Before he replied however he punched me in the lip causing it to bleed.

The driver then told me he was a Taxi Driver and that he was in a hurry to get his passenger to the Airport. On getting back into his Taxi I decided to give him something to think about as my punch sent him across to the passenger side of his vehicle. I then watched as the vehicle kangaroo hopped down the roadway. By now my lip was a mess and swollen. When I walked back to the Police vehicle, my offsider was still under the dashboard. 'What the hell are you still doing under there?' I said. 'I see nothing' came the reply. As we drove back to the Police office my offsider stated that 'You should get something on that lip' 'That's all right' I said, 'You should see the other guy'

Not all my accidents ended up in punch ups or in RAAF Police vehicles. The majority of my accidents were in my own private vehicle. As I found that my little Morris Minor 1000 could not handle the pushing and shoving on the roadway, especially against the big Mercedes vehicles, I opted for a big Ford Fairmont sedan which I purchased from the Manager of the Bosh Company, on the Island. This Ford had been imported from Australia, had a big 6 cylinder engine and tough bumpers, just what I needed. I loved the vehicle until the Malaysian Government decided to increase the registration for big vehicles to around 700 Australian dollars for 6 months registration. I then chose a 1962, four cylinder Volvo Sedan. I was so impressed with this old vehicle that I am still a Volvo owner today.

Another accident involving a RAAF Police vehicle which I was driving, I consider not my fault; however as the Police vehicle was damaged I had to fill out a vehicle accident report, which was then added to my list of accidents. I was working on the mainland at Butterworth and I had just pulled out of the Married Quarters area onto the main Alor Setar roadway which ran past the base. I had stopped at the set of traffic lights not far from the married quarter's area. In front of me, at the lights, was a large truck with a huge canvas covered back. While I was waiting for the lights to change, the back flap of the vehicle was opened and a large marble tile was thrown out, bouncing on the bonnet of my Commodore. This was quickly followed by another tile, then another. The bonnet of my Commodore was a mess. I quickly got out of my vehicle; pulled back the flap grabbed the offender by the throat and pulled him clear of the vehicle. Not getting a lot of sense out of him (probably because I had him by the throat and that his feet were not touching the ground) I took him around to the driver's side of the truck, pulled the driver from the vehicle and banged both their heads together. At the same time demanding to know what the bloody hell was going on as to the damage caused to my Police Vehicle.

Unfortunately the poor driver of the truck had never seen the guy that I pulled from the back of his vehicle, in his life. Ops. It would appear that when the driver of the truck had stopped somewhere this nutter had climbed into the back of his truck and decided to throw out his new marble tiles.

Malaysia appeared not to have any lunatic asylums; nutters were left in the streets, put on the train to Thailand or given a step through (motorcycle) to drive around Malaysia. The local police would put any of their real problem people on the Butterworth train to Thailand. Thailand in turn would send them back to Malaysia. True story, lot of nutters on that train. Irrespective of my dry wit, I love Malaysia, and its people, otherwise I would not have put my life on the line to help free the country of Communist Insurgents and the Indonesian Army.

When I was driving my wife to the markets in Penang one morning, we were in our own private vehicle, the Ford Fairmont. Everywhere I drove through the markets I encountered this old Indian chap, on his black ladies bicycle. All he would do was wave at me, take his feet off of the bicycle pedals, turn around and laugh. He was beginning to get up my nose. I said to my wife that; 'If this little bugger does not get out of my way and stop bothering me, I will run over him' 'That would be a bit hard to do' she said 'As you have hooked the rear guard of his bicycle to the front of the Ford' 'Everywhere you go he will go' Problem solved, speed up then halt suddenly. Bicycle and rider last seen riding off into the sunset.

With my reputation behind the wheel of a motor vehicle, getting worse, no one really wanted to drive with me, even my own two sisters, who came up to Malaysia for a holiday, would only go out if my wife drove. No sense of adventure these women, and both ex-Army. At one time I would drive my boss, the Provost Officer, to and from work, especially when we were working day shift together, at Butterworth. We were both living on the Island at the time however he moved to the mainland after about a year. Not sure if my driving convinced him. It all came to a crunch (excuse the pun) one afternoon when I drove him home from Butterworth. We were heading towards the vehicle Ferry when I overtook a large truck; it was safe to do so as there was no oncoming traffic. As I was passing the truck, one of the local road sweepers decided to sweep the roadway in front of me with his stick broom that they use. 'Bloody hell, you were pretty close to the side of that truck.' Said the boss. 'That's nothing' I said 'See that stick, caught on the front of the car, that's the road sweepers broom'

When I first started driving my boss to work, he used to have his window down, elbow resting on the side of the door and if not telling jokes, he would sing away. After a short period of time driving with me, it was window up, seatbelt tight, no songs or jokes, just bloody big eyes the size of saucers

My stunt driving came to a halt one day after I decide not to let another vehicle pull in front of mine, as there was nowhere for his vehicle to fit. To get the drivers attention I used my police baton to tap on his motor vehicle. There was also a bloody big truck coming the other way as well. Not appreciating the courteous suggestion, by me pointing to the oncoming vehicle, he took the details of my Police vehicle and reported me to my Superiors.

I had to report to the Provost Officer the following day to explain my actions with my Police baton, the day before. I was advised that I was a guest in Malaysia, an Ambassador for my country and that I was in Malaysia to prevent Traffic Accidents, not to bloody well cause them. I was also told to remove the series of little tri-shaws that I had painted on the door of my private motor vehicle, as I was not a bloody Air Ace. He was a terrific boss and I got the message loud and clear as for the next two years I had no further accidents. Err, maybe one more but I am sure that I never went anywhere near his pushbike, honest.

I was again on mobile patrol somewhere in the back streets of Georgetown; I was informed by my offsider that I had clipped a cyclist. 'When, where?' I said 'I felt nothing, how do you know I clipped a bicycle?' 'Because that is his wire basket, from his bicycle, that you have on the front of the Police vehicle' On looking back in the rear vision mirror of the vehicle I watched as this little local, who had been straddling his girls bicycle, lay the bicycle gently down, then lay down beside it, on the roadway. On walking back to the bicycle rider to see why he was lying down, as he was not injured, the little shit would not get up off of the roadway for anything less than 5 ringgit. And to add insult to injury he wanted his wire basket back.

Anyway I was no longer an aggressive driver, but that did not stop members from telling me that they would drive the vehicle if we needed to go out on patrol. Probably why I had no more accidents. I was however, the expert, when it came to filling out the local police traffic accident reports. As you only had about ten lines on the form it was difficult for most people to describe the traffic accident. I had it down pat, I thought of having a rubber stamp made however I don't think the local police would have seen the funny side. For those people wondering about how you went about vehicle insurance, there wasn't any on vehicles over two years old. A lot of the RAAF families drove bombs anyway. Every time that I attended the local police office in connection with RAAF Police business, I was handed a Traffic Accident Form, "Just in case" Bloody cheek, they probably used them for toilet paper anyway, they weren't much good for anything else.

During the first 18months of my tour of Malaysia, with the RAAF, I worked on Butterworth, travelling each day on the Ferry from Penang. I enjoyed my time at Butterworth as for the first 9 months I was employed as a Duty Security Controller and then 9 months in the Criminal Investigation Section. The office of the Duty Security

Controller involved shift work and occasionally, very late at night or early in the morning I would get a bit bored if there was nothing happening on the Police radios. The radios that we had in the office covered the Butterworth mobile patrol and the Penang mobile patrol. The RAAF Police office in the main gate guard room, from where we operated, had a rather large glass window, overlooking the front desk of the Malaysian Military Police who were in charge of the Security at the main gate. The glass window was designed so that we could see out but no one could see back into our office. I used to get a bit tired of watching the Malay guards sitting on each other's lap and combing each other's hair. It turned me off really. I would go out, find out who was the only person who was supposed to be on duty behind the desk, and then tell the remainder to nick off. During the early hours of the morning I would wait for the guard behind the desk to fall asleep, like most times and I would then sneak out and collect all their M16 rifles from their rifle rack, and hide them. I would then sit back and watch the sheer panic, the following morning, when someone woke up to the fact that all their rifles were missing.

During our shift in the Office it was also our duty to check, at regular intervals, on any prisoner that we had in the cells, within the guard room. We never had that many Airmen in cells during the time that I was there; I can only recall one possible drunk. It was also our duty to check on any prisoners that the Malays had in the prison. We had the left hand side of the cell room for our people while the Malays had the right hand cells for their prisoners. We had to keep the cells separate because our hygiene was a little different to theirs. Chicken bones in the sink did not go down too well with the boss. I remember this night that I had one Malay prisoner to check on during my shift, however when I went to check on him I found five naked males in the one cell, with the prisoner. All five were the Military police and I had to ask which one was the prisoner.

Another night when I was on duty, the Malaysian Military Police sent in to me, a Norwegian sailor from one of the visiting ships. I knew there had to be a reason for the Malay Military Police passing him on to me. This guy was not only wearing a long sleeve polar neck pullover, in the Malaysian heat, he was not on the same planet, not my planet anyway. The Norwegian stated that he had just been released from a space ship from where he had been kidnapped. He went about describing the inside of the space ship and of the experiments carried out on him. He kept asking me to feel his pulse and I kept telling him that I did not want to feel his bloody pulse. This guy was spaced out alright, not from a space ship but by some drugs that he had taken. I shipped him off to the base hospital; they took one look at him and turned him out. We had our characters; I still think most of them rode step throughs (motorcycles)

While working in the Criminal Investigation Section, which was attached to the Main Guard room, part of our duty was to ensure that the items in the Police Exhibit Register were accounted for at all times. As I was given the responsibility of the register I decided to check on all the exhibits that we had given the local Police, as evidence to be used for any pending prosecutions. Some of the exhibits like, 10 speed pushbikes, video recorders etc, which had been stolen from Airmen on the Base, had been recorded in the exhibit book for some time. It was common knowledge that we would never get any Locals to court for any offence committed against the RAAF. The offenders would simply come up with some excuse as to why they could not attend court, and this would continue until all the witnesses against them had returned to Australia. I then decided to ask the local Police to return all of our exhibits. Not in your dreams, as all the exhibits had disappeared, never to be seen again. I then stopped giving out any exhibits to anyone outside the RAAF. The equipment stolen on a daily basis from the base, like toilet paper, hand towels, soap, food, etc amounted to hundreds of dollars. The single Airmen, who lived in on the base, were fair game when it came to theft. So were some of the Married Quarters. The only pieces of equipment that were not stolen or tampered with were our Aircraft. This was due to the fact that, once again, the RAAF police dog handlers had the responsibility for Aircraft security, they did a fantastic job.

I recall a visit to Butterworth by an American aircraft, a group calling themselves The Flying Tigers. They were delivering a new radar system for the RMAF (Royal Malaysian Air Force), who owned the base. The aircraft arrived late in the afternoon, and being quite a large aircraft, which had to be unloaded through the nose, the Malays did not have the equipment to unload it. The crew of the aircraft would have to wait until the following day for the Malays to borrow the unloading equipment, from the Australians. On speaking with the American crew I asked them if they were supplying their own security for their aircraft. They said that they would be locking up the aircraft and that none of the crew would be remaining behind. They were off to find the nearest boozer. I suggested that I try and have our RAAF Police dog handlers check the aircraft during the night, but they declined the offer. Imagine their surprise next morning, (not mine) when they found the aircraft broken into, their flying helmets, flying jackets and aircraft parts, missing. They had to wait several days until aircraft parts had to be flown in so that they could fly out. I don't think that they were planning on returning to Butterworth for quite some time.

At times I had some trouble with the local unions and local authorities on the base. The union, (Commonwealth Services Employees Union) always stepped in, if any of their members were interviewed, for any suspected offence, carried out on the base. I remember a day when I placed one of the employees under arrest and escorted him to the guard room, in handcuffs. You would have thought I had stolen the crown jewels as the local paper was contacted and all hell broke loose. The heading in the Straits Times read "Locals see red over actions of RAAF cops." I still have the newspaper cutting. As far as I was concerned a thief is a thief and no one is beyond the law, not even the locals. Made life interesting.

Before I move on to some of the funny incidents that I remember while working on the Island of Penang I should mention some of the everyday encounters with the local population, besides running them over with my motor vehicle, of course. Malaysia has improved immensely since I lived there in 1965 -67 and 1981-84. I hope so anyway.

THE LOCAL MALAY POLICE

The RAAF Police had a good liaison with the local Malay Police, I know I did, I was well known because of my traffic accidents. As the RAAF Police, RAAF Emergency Services etc provided assistance to the locals when needed, (Traffic Accidents, First Aid etc) I found it difficult to understand how I could come across an accident scene involving the locals, turn around, administer first aid if needed, direct traffic to stop further accidents and then as a last resort call our RAAF ambulance service to attend. All the while, a young Malay Policeman would stand on the footpath and observe me. I was later to learn that the Police Officer on foot patrol was not responsible for Motor Traffic Accidents. Pretty bloody stupid situation if you ask me. It was therefore not uncommon to wait for up to 3 hours for the Traffic Police to arrive to take over the situation and then they would only carry out their duty if you drove off in disgust. It was also not uncommon to wait 1-2 hours for a local Ambulance to arrive at a Traffic Accident and what would really astound me was that there was nothing in the rear of the ambulance other than 3-4 males with one old fold up stretcher, about WWII vintage. Then what really shocked me was that if the injured person was not the same nationality as those in the rear of the Ambulance and could not get into the Ambulance by him or herself, then they were left behind. I found this absolutely disgusting. It happened more than once as I attended numerous Traffic Accidents involving injuries during my tour of Malaysia. I would like to think things have improved since I lived there. I will add a short extract here from The West Australian newspaper, dated Tuesday, September 11th, 2007. Dangerous ambulances: Malaysia's ambulances are a health hazard, with dangerous driving and poor maintenance contributing to a worrying number of fatal and serious crashes, a report has found. The Auditor-General also found that ambulances were used to carry food and staff and that vital equipment such as cardiac monitors and ventilators did not work. And you thought I was joking.

AUTOPSIES

It was normally requested that a RAAF Police member be present when an Autopsy was required to be carried out on a RAAF Member. Who required it I do not know. Requests like this did not worry me as I have lost count of the number of dead bodies that I have seen during my Military career, especially involving three Asian wars and 16 years as a Policeman. Also most RAAF Police courses ended with a trip to the morgue, normally after lunch. I guess I just switch off. Again Malay autopsies are nothing like ours, pretty primitive really. I remember one autopsy that I attended at Butterworth; the operating table was a concrete slab, a garden hose on the floor to wash everything away and a small hole in the wall to wash everything outside into an open drain.

The Crows would deal with any waste product. As I said very primitive. To make matters worse they never even removed all the guys' clothes. How the hell they could tell what he died from is anyone's guess. Any autopsies required on females would be carried out in Australia. As far as I was concerned all autopsies involving RAAF members should have been carried out in Australia, but who am I, I am just a foot soldier. Now onto a more pleasant subject, Food.

You will remember the first part of this book involving my initial tour of Malaysia with the Australian Army in 1965, that within the first few days of arrival, I received a bad dose of food poisoning. You will recall that I thought that I was going to die. You will also remember that I never ate another Asian meal during the remaining two years that I lived in Malaysia. When I was serving at No 1 Stores Depot RAAF Tottenham, I mentioned having worked with a RAAF Policeman that I called Mr. Asia. I told Mr. Asia that after living in Malaysia and having received a bad dose of food poisoning, I never again, ate any type of Asian meal. Mr. Asia went to great lengths in telling me as to what I was missing out on and invited me to join him and his family for a meal in Little China Town, Melbourne. When we sat down with his family and friends we ended up having a 13 course banquet and I loved every mouthful. Then again, after numerous bottles of rice wine and yum singing, I guess I would have eaten anything. That's how I got bloody food poisoning in the first place.

Other than a sore head I was okay the next day. I therefore could not wait to taste the Asian food when returning to Malaysia 16 years later. I guess my favourite dishes would have to be Crispy rice soup, Chilly crab and Black rice pudding as a desert. I like most Asian food and will try a different menu each time. I am also a bit partial to satay covered in peanut butter. No wonder I put on weight when I lived there. What I used to like about the Chilly crabs was that you would get three large crabs for a single ringgit. You could pig out on 2 ringgit. I ate a lot of curry chicken as well and one of the restaurants that I would use, when on day patrol on Penang, belonged to a local Malay. This chap would sit outside his Restaurant and as you were about to enter he would always want to shake your hand. Unfortunately his hands were always covered in some type of oil so you entered the Restaurant covered in oil and walked up the stairs where the handrail was also covered in oil. You would wash your hands before the meal to remove the oil, wash your hands after the oily meal and avoid the handrail on your way down the stairs only to be met by the owner who insisted on shaking your hand before you left. Nothing would remove this oil except strong soap; therefore you had to be careful not to get it on your uniform or the vehicle upholstery. It was a challenge.

Another favourite eating place, especially at night was The Craven; I suppose you could call it a Restaurant. This place remained open 24 hours a day, seven days a week and had only closed twice in about 40 years. One was the first day of the Japanese Occupation the other was when they left. The owner also owned a Jewellery store. He would spend the day in his Jewellery shop and sleep next to the till in The Craven each night. My usual order, when I ate there, would be a Murtabak, double egg, double onion, (An Indian style pizza) When you saw how this was cooked you would wonder how the hell I did not get another dose of food poisoning. The only saving grace was that the hotplate, that the food was cooked on, was never allowed to cool down as the hotplate was in use 24 hours a day. Because of the amount of eggs cooked at the stove area the egg shells were thrown into a 20 litre container on the floor. When full, the extra shells would fall onto the dirty floor along with some of the egg slime. Every now and again the chap making your Murtabak or anything else, would use the egg flip, from the hotplate, to scrape up some of the sticky dried egg up off of the floor. I would just close my eyes and enjoy my Murtabak.

When I first started eating out in Malaysia I found it difficult to get used to the strong local coffee, especially made with thick condensed milk. There was no fresh milk available in the shops, you could buy sealed carton milk, (Longlife) which you could keep on a shelf until opened, however once opened it had to be stored in the fridge and used. You would have thought that I would have been used to coffee made on condensed milk as I had six years of it in the Army ration packs. Once I acquired a taste for the coffee made on the condensed milk, I enjoyed it, even though you could stand your tea spoon up in it, as the condensed milk was that thick. You would not believe that after drinking my coffee like that for three years I ended up with withdrawal symptoms for about three months, on arrival back in Australia. That is how much of an effect it had on me over three years. During our last year in Malaysia we were able to obtain frozen cartons of New Zealand milk to use on cereals etc, but it still did not prevent me from having an adverse effect to condensed milk on my arrival back in Australia. Strange how you can get used to things without noticing a change.

One of my favourite pastimes, while on mobile patrol on the Island, was to locate a funeral service, especially a Chinese funeral. I think several people died on the Island every day because there was never any shortage of funerals. With most of the Funerals the deceased body would lay in state for about a week or more and the relatives and friends of the deceased would have a wake. They would virtually have a food festival which at times called for pig on a spit, which was my favourite. It was said to be good luck for the Chinese to invite a stranger to the wake, which is what they told me. I did not mind as I knew where I could eat while on shift, during the week. It beat a Restaurant any day, plus it was free. I got to meet friends that I would not have met otherwise and enjoyed the food. If that is their custom who am I to argue, you told me I was an Ambassador for my country, Boss, just doing my Ambassador thing!

I remember the first time that I took my wife to the local fresh food markets in Penang. A little culture shock for her as we only purchased fresh fruit and vegetables. You would not buy your meat from any of the stalls as it was not refrigerated and the hygiene, a little lacking. You could point to a live chicken and they would cut off it head and pluck it for you but my wife could not bring herself to put a death sentence on the poor fowl. You could order other delicacies like fried bats but as that was not our scene, we passed. The fruits available were superb along with some of the vegetables. We tried every fruit except Durian, because of the smell. When I was finally convinced to try some, I held my nose to get it down. It did not taste too bad but a few days later I could smell it coming through my skin. No wonder they do not allow it in Hotels. We again had to draw the line (excuse the pun) at fish, as this also was not on ice or refrigerated. All our meat, fish and chicken were purchased frozen. Our meat, fish and carton milk were imported into Malaysia from New Zealand. Our frozen chicken was purchased from a little Chinese lady who ran a thriving business selling eggs and frozen chickens to the RAAF families.

It was during one of our first visits to the markets that my wife saw a large paper effigy, of what could only be described as a tubby male person. On seeing this giant paper figure she asked one of the local Chinese if they celebrated Guy Fawkes, like we did in Australia. Back came the reply 'Guy Falk's, Guy Falk's, who Guy Falk's'? After taking about ten minutes explaining Guy Fawkes to a blank face, he answered 'No him Hungry Ghost,' to an equally blank face. So that I don't leave you wondering, who the bloody hell is the Hungry Ghost, I will add a paragraph all about the festival. As Halloween is to the Americans, the Hungry Ghost Festival is to the Chinese. The Hungry Ghost Festival is an occasion that is taken very seriously by the Chinese. The festival falls on the 7th month of the lunar New Year. It is celebrated in China, Malaysia, Singapore and other areas with a large Chinese community. It is believed by the Chinese that during this month, the gates of hell are opened to free the hungry ghost who then wander to seek food on Earth.

The reason why the Chinese celebrate this festival is to remember their dead family members and pay tribute to them. They also feel that offering food to the deceased appeases them and may frighten away any bad luck. You have seen Chinese place items of food in their little temples. Not Bloody Guy Fawkes.

CHAPTER 34

RECREATION FOR FAMILIES IN MALAYSIA

RAAF Police members of Penang and Butterworth Patrols 1981 – 1984. Author front row, first on right.

I could not possibly list all of the Recreation activities that were available to the RAAF families while serving in Malaysia, anyway a long list of anything is boring and I am a one finger typist. Malaysia was what you made it; you either enjoyed it or hated it. I feel sorry for those people who did not enjoy their time in Malaysia. Every recreation activity was available in Malaysia. Our RAAF Police Section, even though shift workers managed a team in A, B and C Grade Volley Ball,

Softball, and Darts. Badminton was a popular game as we had our own courts at the RAAF Centre. Normal activities like Swimming was also available both on the mainland and the Island as well. Ten Pin Bowling was another popular activity along with sailing, as Butterworth had its own boat club. A lot of activities could also be carried out at the RAAF Centre on the Island. This area contained our RAAF Police Office, RAAF Hospital, Barracks section, living quarters for the single Airmen living on the Island, NAAFI Store, Barber, Restaurant and much more. A self-contained RAAF unit.

Due to the value of the Australian dollar at the time, about three Malay ringgit, to the Aussie Dollar, there was always a party being held at one of the RAAF Police member's homes, RAAF friends place or at a Locals residence. Most of the times you would have the party catered for because food was just so cheap. We purchased our Alcohol through the NAAFI Store which was reasonably priced compared to local prices. A litre, cask of wine, which we were buying in Australia for about $4-$5, would cost anything up to 70 Ringgit Malay, if purchased in country.. We would have the wine casks flown up from Australia by our RAAF Transport and whoever was organizing the delivery, would add their clubs profit to the price. It still worked out a lot cheaper than buying wine locally. If you did not want to have a party at your home you could attend one of the local Holiday Resorts on the Island, to celebrate an event. We celebrated Christmas Day at one of the Resorts where the function was fabulous. We also enjoyed Christmas in Singapore where we would celebrate Christmas Day in the old Raffles Hotel.

What my wife and I enjoyed most were the Fancy Dress parties, these were held at private homes as well as at the RAAF Centre. I would make up costumes for my wife and myself and any of our children who happened to be visiting on School holidays. I am a whiz on an over locker and made many an interesting costume.

One of our Fancy Dress parties was held at the home of our

Warrant Officer, RAAF Police. He and his wife were a lovely couple and perfect host. The theme of the party was Monster Night and the costumes made up by some of the members were terrific.

One member came as a Monny Monster (Monsoon Drain Monster) though I think I met his mate as one of the local beggars. He had covered himself in some kind of grease and everywhere he sat he left this greasy/oily spot. It took him days to get rid of all the grease from his body. He looked unusual in his RAAF uniform with black greasy ears. The costume that I made for my wife was that of the Bat Lady, with a black flowing winged cape and the mask of a bat. My stepson went as an Executioner with a full mask to cover his face and a big double blade axe to lop off heads. They looked terrific. I went as a Mummy, straight out of a Tomb.

My wife had wrapped me up with about 30 large bandages that we bought for the occasion. About an hour before the party I stripped down to my jocks while my wife wrapped me in the bandages. In between the bandages I placed the odd, big rubber worm. While I remained standing and the bandages tight, everything looked terrific. I did not think about sitting down or having to drive to the party. We must have looked a site driving along the road. While driving, I noted that I needed petrol, so I had to pull into a petrol station. I do not know what the attendant was thinking, seeing a Mummy at the bowser and a car full of other weird people. By the time I arrived at the party all my bandages had come loose and within half an hour I lost them all and had to borrow a pair of shorts from our host. At another Fancy dress party my wife went as a Scare Crow and I stuffed all the ends of her costume with straw, only to cause her to break out in a rash, the next day. I went along as a Samurai Warrior with false hair/moustache, only to have the guests ask my wife as to why, I was not at the party and was I working? They were fun nights as you can see by some of the fancy dress photographs in this book. Malaysia was what you made it, great times and fond memories to look back on.

RAAF Police – Family – Fancy Dress parties in Malaysia 1981-1984. Above – Authors wife Joy, left, Mrs. Perry centre and Author right. Below – Author in bandages, which later fell off, standing with Stepson Tony.

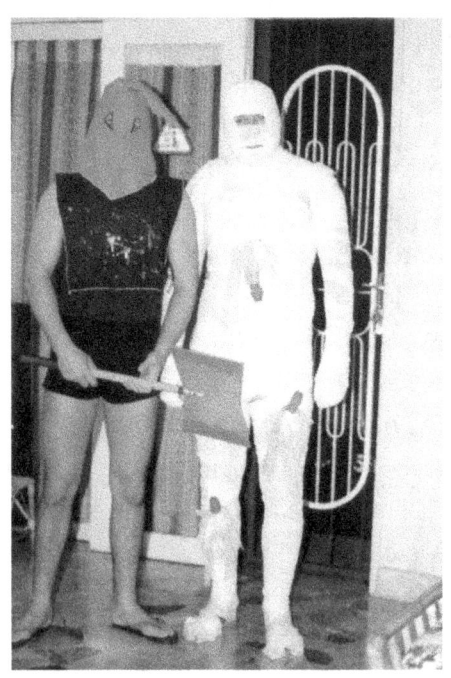

Local Snake Charmer – Butterworth and Penang. Great attraction at children's parties – when asked to help remove Cobra Snakes from the RAAF Married Quarters he was never available

The Authors daughter, Tanya, above and two boys below, on a school holiday visit to Penang, in 1983.

`RAAF Police members of Penang and Butterworth Patrols 1981 – 1984. Author front row, third in from left.

' Hurry up take the Bloody photo as I don't like Snakes.' The Author – Penang Malaysia 1982.

CHAPTER 35
PENANG SHIFT SUPERVISOR

After serving my time working at Butterworth I was employed on Penang as a Shift Supervisor for 11 months and the following 9 months, as the Sergeant in charge of the RAAF Police. I enjoyed my time on Penang as I did not have to travel across to Butterworth, on the Ferry, each day. There was always something to do on shift. The following events that I intend to mention which took place on the Island are in no particular order because I have no bloody idea when they took place. What I do remember is that when I first started my first shift on the Island, our Police vehicle was a Holden Commodore Station wagon. I remember this because the back seat of the vehicle was folded down and this large, clear Perspex shield took up all the space in the back. When I asked what the big piece of Perspex was doing in the back of the Wagon, I was informed, by one of the Corporals, that it was used to remove Cobra snakes from out of the married quarters. As I don't like snakes of any sort I let the matter rest. Believing that, as a Senior NCO on the Island I would not be required to remove snakes, (Give the snake removing job to the next Corporal that walks through the door) I could not believe how wrong I was, as rank had no privileges in Malaysia when the job had to be done.

It did not take long before a request to remove a snake from a married quarter, was received, when I just happened to be on duty. I dreaded this request and considered taking along the 12 gauge shotgun as a backup.

On arrival at the residence, my Police partner, who had been on the Island for some time and had removed snakes previously, removed the shield from the back of the vehicle. Someone went to a lot of bother to design this shield, unfortunately they had been born in the wrong era;

Romans and Gladiators would have been at home behind this thing. The shield was approximately 2mm thick, stood just under 2 meters high and about 1 meter wide. In the centre of the shield you had an elaborate handle which the Romans would have been proud of. The weight of the bloody thing was incredible.

On standing behind the shield, which towered over my head, I asked my offsider as to how the shield was used to remove snakes. He said 'What you do is approach the snake while behind the shield and when you get close enough you reach around and hit the snake with your baton.' I said 'Are you serious?' 'Whose stupid bloody idea was this?' 'The boss,' he said 'He is worried about the spitting Cobras.' 'Spitting Cobras, Spitting Cobras, what bloody Spitting Cobras?'

The shield and I lasted five minutes. The weight, width and height of the bloody thing made it difficult to manoeuvre in the house let alone a small room. Failing that, I needed another meter added to my arm and the same with my baton. I had a lesser chance of being bitten or spat at without the shield. Maybe if you were lucky enough to drop the shield on the snake and jump on both, you had a chance. Not much bloody good when the snake is under the bed. When I took over as Sergeant in charge of the RAAF Police on the Island the shield somehow disappeared, probably in the bottom of the Penang harbour.

Our solution to removing snakes from the married quarters and prevent them from spitting at us, was to approach them with the biggest CO_2 fire extinguisher that you could find and freeze them. It made one hell of a mess in the home, but hell it got the job done. I would have made a bigger mess with the 12 gauge. The wife of my boss, god bless her, never called the Police to remove snakes from her home, she would just push the little buggers out the door, by flicking them with one of the local rice stick brooms. Not this boy, if I had my way I would have used the Fire Department, axes and all. I did not volunteer to remove snakes, especially Cobra snakes, as you would imagine, however I would not have missed the experience for the world.

Other than the odd snake, Monkeys sometimes became a problem, especially in and around the RAAF School on the Island. The main concern was that monkeys can carry Rabies. A few of the RAAF families had Monkeys for pets, not my bloody pet when you had to deal with them. I had enough trouble with them when they kept going through my rubbish bin and making one hell of a mess in the yard. The little shits. My boss had a pet monkey and every time you approached it, it would steal whatever was in the top pocket of your uniform and nick off, you had a devil of a time to retrieve your possessions.

I think he must have bought it from a local who trained it to rob tourist. While on duty one afternoon I received a call from the Principal of the RAAF School, who advised me that the large tree, in the centre of the school, was full of monkeys. The Principal further stated that the monkeys had become aggressive and had attacked the odd kid, for his or her lunch. I thought about how I was going to resolve the problem and called the local authorities to obtain permission to shoot the monkeys, as a last resort. I was informed that I could not shoot the monkeys however they would send someone out to resolve the problem. Whatever that meant.

The following day two locals arrived sporting a 12 gauge shotgun each. I asked them what they were going to do to resolve the monkey problem within the school grounds and they said that they were going to shoot all of the monkeys. I asked them not to destroy the monkeys while the children were about and could they wait until they were in class or when they were not at school. There was also the safety of the children to consider as well. They agreed not to destroy the monkeys until all of the children were in class. I left the area a short time later on another call.

I had not gone long before I was informed that our Monkey Munchers had gone into the school grounds, right on school recess, with guns blazing. When I arrived back the scene was like something out of the "Ok Corral." They not only demolished all the monkeys in the tree, they demolished the tree as well. There were bits of monkey and tree everywhere. I was devastated, along with the kids. The School had to bring in Trauma Counselors for the children. We never again asked for the monkeys to be destroyed, not while I was there.

I remember one bad experience that I had with a monkey, was when I was asked by a lady to help catch her pet monkey after it had escaped from a cage at her residence. The monkey had entered one of the bedrooms in the house and was starting to damage items within the room. When I entered the room this ferocious little shit attacked me, clawing the hell out of my arms and face. Some bloody pet, not my pet. I left the monkey in the room and told the lady to leave it and when it became hungry and thirsty, it would behave itself. A few days later the woman rang me to tell me that the plan had worked however the monkey demolished the room and tore the curtains to shreds. I informed her that my other solution would have made a bigger mess, as I would have used the 12 gauge shotgun on him if the little shit attacked me again. Bloody snakes and monkeys, give me kids any day at least I can nail one of their feet to the floor.

The Island as well as the Mainland, at one time, had a serious problem with crows. They were that bad that the Government offered one Malaysian Ringgit for every crow destroyed. This was unusual because Malaysia still had Communist Insurgents and the carrying of weapons by the locals was outlawed. However everyone now seemed to be sporting a shotgun. It was a dangerous time to be around locals with shotguns as we ended up with damaged windscreens as well as windows. I could not understand as to how anyone was going to make money out of killing crows, as shotgun shells cost one Malaysian Ringgit each and a dead crow worth one Malaysian Ringgit

It did not solve the problem as the crows flourished. If Malaysia had insisted that all food scraps were to be placed in rubbish bins instead of all over the place, then they would not have had a crow problem.

While carrying out office duties one afternoon in the RAAF Police office on Penang, I again received a telephone call from the Principal of the RAAF school. I was informed that a local male had entered the school grounds, removed his clothes and stood naked in front of some school children. It was a common occurrence for some of the local males to expose themselves to school children. The children attending the RAAF School were escorted to and from the school, by bus, each day, to ensure their safety. On arriving at the school I could not locate our flasher however on carrying out a search of the area, I found him, still naked, sitting under a tap in the front yard of a RAAF married quarter, just down the road from the school. He had the tap running and was playing with the water. Located nearby was what was left of a dirty old pair of trousers which had been held up with a piece of rope. When I tried to get him up so that I could put on his trousers he took off, running down the side of the married quarter and into the back yard, with me in hot pursuit. As we entered the back yard the lady of the house, or Amah, was pegging out bed sheets on the back clothes line. As the nude male and I ran in and out between the sheets, the lady, who still had a clothes peg in her mouth, never wavered in her actions as she quietly went about her duties. Almost as if this was an everyday occurrence. When I finally tackled our naked man I took him back to the front of the married quarter so that I could get him to put on his trousers. As I arrived at the front of the home, the entire School assembly was hanging out of the School windows, clapping. As I was not sure as to the state of mind of the offender, and being alone on the job, I decided to handcuff his hands behind his back. This did not, however, prevent him from removing his trousers again, once I placed him in the back of my patrol vehicle.

I drove to the local Penang Police station to deliver the offender, only to find that I had left my handcuff keys sitting on the desk in my office. I then decided to go back to my office with the offender, to collect my handcuff keys. As I pulled up outside the RAAF Police office, the Provost Officer was walking out of the front door. On looking inside my vehicle and seeing the naked man, he did an about turn, heading straight back into the Office mumbling something about 'Wheels again' I took the offender to the local Police and advised them what had taken place, I watched, as the offender combed the hairs on his legs. I knew by the tone of the Police, that they did not intend to do anything about the offender exposing himself to School children. About an hour later while carrying out further patrols of the area, I again saw the offender, half naked, wandering the streets. All in a day's work, the fruit loops were everywhere.

RAAF Police members of Penang and Butterworth Patrols 1981-1984

Entrance to Air Base Butterworth Malaysia

RMAF Security Members

RAAF Police Security Patrol Office Butterworth Malaysia 1981 – 1984

RAAF F111 Aircraft above – RAAF Mirage Aircraft below RAAF Air Base Butterworth Malaysia 1981 – 1984

Royal Malaysian Air Force (RMAF) F5 E Jets Air Base Butterworth Malaysia 1981-1984. Below – RMAF F5 E – Crashed during take off Pilot – Mejar (Udara) Victor Emanuel – escaped unhurt.

Normal – every day, Traffic Accidents, involving Locals, either at Butterworth or Penang, at which the RAAF Police would assist, if first on the scene – none of these Traffic Accidents were mine, by the way.

Above – Malaysian Motorcycle Police – we called them 'CHIPS' after the American TV series. Below – normal – every day, Traffic Accident, involving Locals in Malaysia.

RAAF Police Office on Penang Island, Malaysia during the time that the RAAF was Stationed in Malaysia. Below – the Author outside the RAAF Police Office, Penang 1983.

Our first RAAF Married Quarter in Malaysia 1981 – 3J Medan Lembah Permai, Tanjong Bungah, Penang Malaysia. We lived in this residence for two years before moving to Vale Tempe, Penang in1984. Below – our first motor vehicle purchased in Malaysia, a Morris Minor 1000, no rust, ran well and cost $200 Australian, to buy. My wife and I still own a Morris Minor 1000 today.

Murtabak is an Indian styled pizza filled with ground mutton and onions. The 'Chanai' is a plain pizza eaten with dhall curry. This was where I ate breakfast most mornings when on Penang Patrol – the Author.

CHAPTER 36
LETTERS OF APPRECIATION/ THANKS

During my tour of duty in Malaysia I received several letters of thanks in assisting RAAF Family members and the RAAF School Teachers. I also received two commendations from the Officer Commanding RAAF Butterworth. I was just doing my job however it was nice to receive the letters of thanks, which I will always treasure.

One such letter I received from an Australian school teacher, employed by the Australian Government, to teach our children while they were living in Malaysia. I first met this school teacher at the Penang General Hospital. I received a radio message while on mobile patrol that an Australian male had been assaulted by several locals and had been taken to Penang General. On attending the hospital and on making enquiries as to the Australian, I was directed to a male person lying on the floor, in the hallway of the hospital. Several local people were also lying on the floor with injuries. When I tried to communicate with the Australian I found that he was bleeding from head injuries and was in a coma. When I asked if a doctor had seen the Australian I was informed that they were still waiting for a doctor. When I asked if the Australian had been given any type of medication, I was told that he had not asked for any. As the guy was in some type of coma and could not be woken up I found it quite easy to understand as to why he had not asked to be treated. I was concerned at not being able to wake him and the blood dripping from his head wound.

I radioed through to the RAAF Medical Centre and advised them of the situation. I was informed that I needed to seek medical attention for him right away because if he could not be woken from a coma he may suffer brain damage as a result. The Medical Centre stated that they were sending an Ambulance however it would be of great assistance if I could meet them half way with the injured male if a doctor could not see him immediately. As I was informed by one of the local nurses that she could not tell me when a doctor would be available, I took it upon myself to have the injured Australian laid out in the back of my Station Wagon. I then made my way towards the RAAF Medical Centre, all the while staying in radio contact with the oncoming RAAF ambulance. The Penang Hospital was a reasonable distance from the RAAF medical centre. About half way between the two hospitals I transferred my patient to the waiting Ambulance. I found out several days later that had I not made contact with the RAAF Hospital and taken it upon myself to transfer the injured Australian to the RAAF Hospital, he may have died or suffered permanent brain damage. The letter of thanks I received from the School Teacher for saving his life and the Commendation from the Officer Commanding, RAAF Base Butterworth, I treasure very much.

At another time I received a lovely letter of thanks from an elderly lady, and I mean a lady. I will refer to her as "Granny." Granny was one tough little lady, I could not help admire her courage. Granny was in Malaysia for a holiday and visiting her daughter, who was one of the RAAF school teachers. Granny was shopping in Georgetown, Penang, with her daughter, when two locals on a motorcycle tried to snatch her handbag as they drove by. Granny had her handbag, on a long strap across her shoulder when the offenders tried to remove it from her. Granny was not going to give up her handbag that easily and stood her ground. However the two guys on the motorcycle pulled her off her feet and dragged her, on her back, along the roadway. Granny would still not let go of her handbag even with injuries to her back and sides. She managed to pull the pillion passenger, who was holding onto her handbag, off of the rear of the motorcycle. The driver of the motorcycle then lost control of the bike and ran into a nearby stall. Locals nearby, who had seen what happened jumped on the two offenders and were holding them down, as my offsider and I arrived on the scene. In the meantime Granny lay on the road bleeding from her injuries and in shock. She still had her handbag and could still raise a smile. I arranged for a RAAF ambulance to take Granny to the Penang Medical Centre, as evidence of her injuries, had to be collected by the local authorities.

After Granny had been seen by a local doctor at the Penang Hospital and photographs taken of her injuries, my offsider and I arranged for her to be transferred to the RAAF Medical Centre. I visited Granny after my shift and took her some flowers. The two offenders, responsible for injuring Granny, had been handed over to the Penang Police and I was to attend the Police station the next day, to enquire about their charges.

On attending the Penang Police station the following day, I spoke to the Inspector who was handling the case. I knew the Inspector from previous dealings involving local offenders. The Inspector asked me to follow him into a room, where the two offenders were being held. The Inspector said 'You realize Sergeant that you will never get these two to court in connection with the assault on the elderly lady?' I said 'I realize that Sir, but I can only try and push the matter through as hard as I can.' 'I have a better solution, one which I hope you can explain to the lady concerned and I hope she will be satisfied.' With that he told the two offenders to place their hands on the table, palms down. 'That could have been my mother that you pulled along the street and injured, you bloody cowards.' Said the Inspector. Before I could blink, he smashed the table four times, with his police baton. As the two offenders screamed in pain, I realized he had broken all the fingers of their hands. 'They won't be stealing anymore handbags or riding a bike, for a while.' Said the Inspector. I was stunned as well as shocked. 'Please advise the lady of what has happened to the offenders and please pass on our apologies as for her being injured, while visiting our Country.' 'I hope she makes a speedy recovery.' Said the Inspector.

Justice was swift and slightly out of the ordinary, but hell who was I to argue with local Authorities.

Granny sent me a lovely letter, along with appreciation expressed by her family, thanking me and my offsider for taking time out to look after her, as she was not a member of the RAAF. She did not have to worry as the RAAF went out of its way to assist anyone in Malaysia, all part of being a good Ambassador for our Country.

Another day another early morning patrol around the Island. I had about three hours of my shift remaining when I received a call that one of our Airmen had been involved in an accident on his way to work. It was about 0500 hours (5am) when I arrived at the scene. The Airman had been riding to work on his pushbike when a local walked out in front of him, causing a collision, whereas, both were knocked to the ground. The Airman was okay, sustaining only a few cuts and some bruising. The local however, was still sitting on the ground holding his right knee with both hands and rocking to and fro. At the same time asking for money, in between his ooos and arrs. I recognized the local immediately, he was a local identity we called Captain Pyjamas. 'What's wrong with you Captain?' I asked. 'Where are you hurt?' 'Ooh arr, you give me money, ooh arr' was all that I was getting out of the Captain.

I called for a RAAF Ambulance to convey Captain Pyjamas to the Penang General Hospital. Once Captain was safely on his way to hospital I went about my normal duties until my shift finished. Imagine my shock the following afternoon when I commenced my shift and on being told that Captain Pyjamas had died within about two hours of him being delivered to the Penang Hospital. The Captain, when accepted by the Hospital, had been left in the hallway, without being attended to by a Doctor. The Captain died of a skull fracture. He must have hit his head on the ground when struck by the pushbike. Why he was holding his knee when I put him in the Ambulance is anyone's guess. His family or relations, who should have been looking after him in the first place, were now wanting to contact me, and for me, to pay some type of compensation. What for, I do not know, as I did not kill him.

I missed seeing Captain Pyjamas, walking around the area. He was a local identity. How he was given the name of Captain Pyjamas, was that he always wore a long set of fleecy lined, pin striped, pyjamas. The pyjamas were of red and white stripes and had faded with time and dirt. How he stood the heat of Malaysia while living in winter pyjamas, I do not know. When you approached Captain Pyjamas in uniform and spoke to him, he would salute you, hence our name for him.

The Captain had a bad habit of just entering your property to look for any bottles that you may have lying around your yard. As most RAAF married quarters had dogs, the Captain would possibly be attacked by the dogs, however this did not deter him as he would always get his bottles, dog hanging off him or not.

It was not uncommon to be left lying in the Foyer of the Penang General Hospital for hours on end, before being seen by a Doctor. Captain Pyjamas was not the first or the last person to die in the foyer of the hospital. Our hospital system in Australia may have run down a little over the years but it has never been as bad as some overseas countries I have visited. I still believe Australia is the best country in the world however I am biased.

CHAPTER 37
GENERAL PATROLS AROUND PENANG

The main purpose of the RAAF Police on Penang and at Butterworth was to protect and serve the RAAF members, their families and any personnel attached to the RAAF, including the civilian School Teachers. Once the personnel had been taken care of then your next priority was to the security of RAAF property. To carry out these duties the RAAF Police would carry out patrols 24 hours a day, seven days a week. Patrols were never dull and it would be unlikely that you ever had a quiet or boring shift.

The object of the patrols on Penang was to check on the security of all the known married quarters and once that was completed you would possibly venture into town and check out some of the back alleys of Georgetown. The reason that the back alleys were checked was that these areas were out of bounds to all RAAF Personnel. The back alleys were not very nice places to visit as there had been the odd murder, serious assault and robbery, known to have taken place.

When a new RAAF Police member went out with you on his first patrol, especially on Penang, you would ensue that he did not drive and that he sat in the front passenger seat of the vehicle. What would take place was that after you drove around for an hour or so the new member would nod off to sleep due to the slow movement of the vehicle and the heat of Malaysia. Once you were sure that the member was asleep, you would drive into one of the known back alleys of Penang, lean over and wind the passenger window down. When the window was wound down, this was the signal for one of the "Shims," in the alley, to race over, grab the new member in a head lock and plant a sloppy kiss on him. Scared the hell out of you if you had ever been caught. You would then be a fully-fledged Patrol Officer. To explain the word "Shim", she and him, is what is known as a transsexual. Men that can't make up their mind as to what they want to be, that is how it was explained to me. Anyway it came as a hell of a shock if you had ever been initiated by having a "Shim" slobber all over you. I have seen members wash themselves in coca cola after having been initiated. Some of the "Shims" were not the most attractive people I had ever met. As I said, Patrols were never boring.

One particular area on the Island, where a row of RAAF married quarters backed on to a large vacant lot, had to be checked out each night and on a regular basis. The vacant lot had been cleared a long time ago to make way for a high rise. When clearing the land the excess soil had been stored alongside the rear fences of several of the RAAF married quarters. The stored soil was about 15 meters high and overlooked about five to six married quarter homes. Thick vegetation had covered the stored soil, making it an ideal place for some of the locals to hide in at night, so that they could look into the windows of the RAAF married quarters. All occupants of the married quarters had been advised to keep the curtains of their quarters closed at night, because of the peeping toms.

When it came to my turn, to carry out night inspections of the area where the locals would hide to peep into the married quarters, I would ensure that I caused havoc among the peeping toms. When I arrived in the area I would enter the vacant lot with all the lights of the Patrol vehicle, off. The peeping toms would leave their motorbikes all parked in a neat row, near to where they were hiding. I would sneak along and remove all the ignition keys from the motorbikes or some wiring, anything to prevent them from being started.

Once I had done this I would race up into the bushes with my baton and tap as many peeping toms on their crash helmets as I could find. The sheer panic this would cause and the fact that they could not get their motorcycles to go was hilarious. Each time I would do this the group of peeping toms would get smaller and smaller until they got the message. To report their actions to the local Police was a waste of time, as the police would not even attend. So it was up to me how I handled the situation, right or wrong, it worked. It made life interesting.

The RAAF Police patrols were well known and respected around Penang and Butterworth. There was a particular street in Georgetown, Penang that on some nights, when you drove into this street, a local Indian lass would come out to greet you, like a long lost friend. What made it unusual was that this Indian girl lived two floors up in a building, where the window of her room, overlooked the street that we would drive into.

On seeing the Patrol Vehicle enter the street, this Indian lass would leap out of the building, through her window; grab hold of the top of the metal lamp post adjacent the window and slide down to the ground. The fact that she did not kill herself or suffer some form of burns to her hands while sliding down this lamp post, was amazing. I have never seen anything like it in my life. This Indian lass would then make her way over to the Patrol Vehicle to say hello. The fact that she was so high on drugs probably explained a lot of things.

I have always been a keen photographer as long as I can remember. The fact that my Father was also a very good photographer with the old box brownie and developed his own photographs probably had something to do with why I am so interested in photography. My daughter, Tanya, is also a very good photographer. I always carried my personal camera with me, whenever I was out on Patrol. This not only allowed me to photograph any important scene in connection with my Police duties, but any unusual scenes that I came across involving the local inhabitants of Malaysia. I particularly liked photographing the Beggars in and around Georgetown. Some people might find this a bit strange but people are fascinating in all walks of life and some of the Beggars had their own peculiarity. To give you an example, I took a photograph of an old Indian Beggar who remained lying in the same position, on a foot path, for the entire three years that I lived in Malaysia. Every now and again the newspaper that this chap was lying on would be replaced with some clean paper. I only ever saw him drink, thick condensed milk and nothing else. He was in a terrible state of health as you can imagine, but he never moved from his position on the foot path the entire time. Had I not photographed him in his position and dated the photographs, no one would believe me that a person could lay in the same position, on a foot path, for three years. I have included a photograph of this Beggar, in this book for you to consider. Another Beggar who would fascinate me would bring his lunch to work, all neatly wrapped in a plastic bag. This chap would hide his lunch and beg for money during the day, however when lunch time came around he would look around to see if anyone was watching and take out his lunch.

On collecting his lunch he would leave his position on the foot path, from where he was begging and move to a table at one of the restaurants. After he finished his lunch he would return to his position on the foot path and continue begging. Not so silly after all. I have included a photograph of him in this book. After three years on Patrol I ended up with a very unusual collection of photographs of Malaysian Beggars.

Rainy days, which were most of the year, saw heavy monsoon rains and some of the locals would come up with some unusual ideas to keep from getting wet, especially when riding their motorcycles. I have seen a family of four, on one motorcycle; wrap themselves up in a large plastic bag, with just their heads sticking out above the plastic, their bodies and the rest of the motorcycle completely covered as they drove along the roadway.

Another time I observed a chap who had placed a large cardboard box over his motorcycle as he drove along the road, in the rain. He simply punched a hole in the box for his head; someone must have placed his crash helmet on his head once he was in the box, because he would not have been able to reach his head with his hands. You could not see the motorcycle, just a wet saggy cardboard box, with a head, as he drove along the road.

Crash helmets for the Malaysian motorcyclists came in all shapes and sizes however if you could not afford one you probably made your own. If there was any law on motorcycle helmets it was never enforced. It was not unusual to see a square plastic ice cream container used as a crash helmet, I kid you not. Another favorite was a toy plastic army combat helmet. All absolutely useless in an accident. At times the original crash helmet would have the inner removed to make two. Many a time you would see mum driving the motorcycle wearing the outer crash helmet, while the child on the back of the motorcycle, wearing the inner piece of the helmet. All foam of course. When the crash helmet was worn with the inner foam removed, the crash helmet itself would float around your head, blocked your vision at times and fell off in an accident. Some of the locals even advertised their trade as crash helmet repairers, along with repairers of fountain pens and anything else they thought they might be skilled in. Some of the trades advertised in the local paper read, coconut plucker, chicken plucker and satay seller. A name like One Thin Thong was also not unusual.

AROUND OUR HOME ON PENANG

My wife Joy and I have always been house proud and love our garden. It was no different with any of the RAAF married quarters that we occupied. We always improved the accommodation, lawns and garden. Each time we vacated a RAAF married quarter we received a letter from the Barracks Officer complementing us on the condition of our MQ. In some cases members working in the Barracks Section would move into our MQ after we vacated. Malaysian RAAF married quarters were no different as we occupied our first MQ in Tanjong

Bungah, Penang and in our last year, we moved to a new RAAF MQ in Vale of Tempe, Penang. At each MQ we put in extra plants/trees along with a barbecue. When you first occupied a RAAF MQ in Malaysia all the local traders beat a path to your door.

You did not have to leave your home for any reason. Even after you were settled in your home your grocery boy would visit twice a day, cobblers would pull up outside you home and make you a set of shoes, tailors would attend and in a few hours come back with your new suit. All types of vendors would attend your home to sell you their wares. The ladies could have music lessons, facials, nails and anything else they required in the privacy of their home. How anyone could not enjoy Malaysia is beyond me.

I remember one funny incident when one of the cake vendors peddled his bicycle along the street opposite our home. The vendor and his wife were well known for their delicious donuts, curry puffs and cream buns. The male vendor would sell the cakes in the afternoon while his wife would sell the cakes in the mornings. The male vendor would wear an old dark blue RAAF cap that someone had obviously given him. The cap was way too big for him and would fall down over his face as he peddled along. The vendor's wife would wear the cap when she sold her cakes in the mornings. The cap was way too big for her as well. This day when the male vendor entered the street he would yell out his wares, 'Donuts, curry puffs, cream buns, donuts curry puffs, cream buns' My neighbour went out to the vendor and asked him for half a dozen curry puffs. The vendor advised my neighbour that he had sold out of curry puffs. 'But you yelled out that you were selling curry puffs.' said my neighbour. 'So solly, so solly' said the vendor' "You should not yell out that you have curry puffs' said my neighbour. 'So solly, so solly' said the vendor. (Not being able to roll his R's) As the vendor peddled away his new sales pitch was 'Donuts, cream buns, Nooo curry puffs, donuts, cream buns, Nooo curry puffs' We had our characters.

Another of the vendors who peddled his bicycle into our street was a tall Indian chap who sold tapioca from a large round can he carried on his bicycle. If you did not supply your own container for the tapioca he would serve it up to you on a banana leaf, using his bare hand. This was of course after he had used the same bare hand to scratch his bare bum under his sarong.

Chinese New Year was a dangerous time to leave the louver windows of your MQ open, as the Chinese would set off sky rockets all over the place, at any time of the day or night. It was not unusual to hear about a home being burnt down after a sky rocket had gone through the window and set fire to the house curtains. Fireworks are banned in Malaysia; however I guess they forgot to tell the Chinese.

Our main bedroom on the top floor of our MQ, had a small balcony which overlooked the street in front of our home. I had a box on the balcony which contained balloons filled with water. I used the water filled balloons to disperse packs of wild dogs and monkeys that would sometimes gather on the roadway outside our home. I remember one morning, about 0300 hours (3am) when I was woken up by a Chinese lady sitting in her Mercedes vehicle, parked in the middle of the street, directly opposite our home. This woman was blasting the horn button of the Mercedes and screaming at a Chinese neighbour. Apparently this woman was third wife of the neighbour and the neighbour was supposed to be with this woman instead of wife number one or two or something.

I screamed out at the woman in the Mercedes that it was 3am in the morning and told her politely to shut up the bloody noise. She took no notice of me, of course and kept on blasting the horn and screaming. I noted that the Mercedes had a sun roof which was open, as from time to time this woman would stand on the vehicle seat and yell out through the sun roof. I decided that I had had enough and several of my water filled balloons found their way into the vehicle through the sun roof. Problem solved as soggy driver drove off into the sunset, never to be heard from again. It was never a dull moment even around the MQ.

I guess I could write an entire book on Malaysia alone as it is such an interesting place however I will finish my tour of Malaysia with the RAAF by mentioning two final episodes.

One being a car rally that I was involved in on Penang and the other, a month long trek with some other RAAF Police through Thailand, Laos and Burma.

To keep my posting to Malaysia in some form of Military Order, I guess it is a good time to mention here that during my three years in Malaysia with the RAAF I returned to Australia on two separate occasions to give evidence at two separate Court Martials, involving Airmen. These hearings were the results of two investigations that I completed prior to my posting to Malaysia. Both resulted in successful prosecutions.

The 'Shims' (He maybe She) of Perlis Street, in Penang, Malaysia – 1981-1984, This Street was out of bounds to all RAAF Personnel, Therefore had to be patrolled, by RAAF Police, on a regular basis.

The 'Shims' of Perlis Street, in Penang, Malaysia 1981-1984. The males/females were harmless enough and had a good liaison with the RAAF Police, as you can tell. There was never any problems with RAAF members entering Perlis Street.

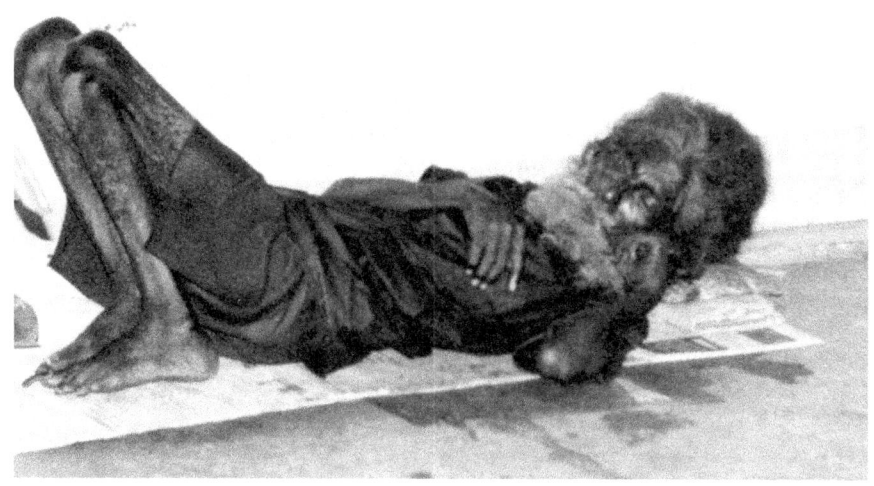

Penang – Beggar – This Beggar remained in the same position, on the foot path, during the entire three years that the Author served in Malaysia, from 1981-1984. He was only ever seen to drink condensed milk and have the paper changed from underneath him.

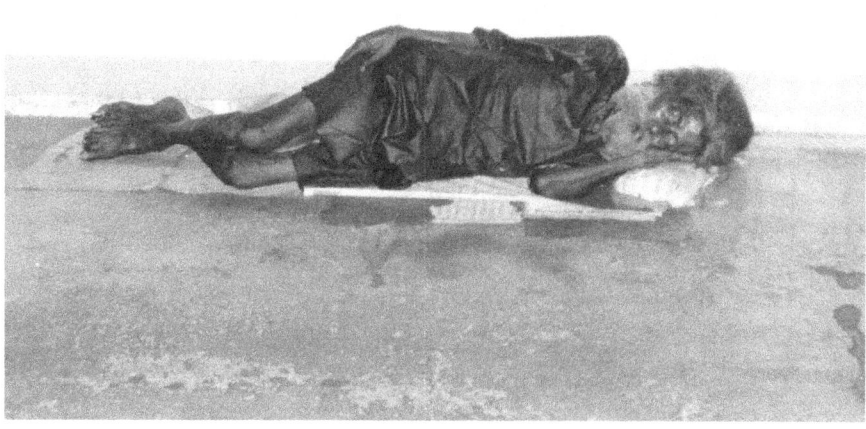

Penang Beggar – known to Author as 'Sandwich Sam' as he would sneak away from begging to have his lunch.

Penang Beggar – known to Author as 'The Saint'.

Penang, Malaysia, Beggars 1981-1984. Check out the beggar's hair style above, and his shoes with no soles. It is hard to imagine such poverty.

Chinese New Year – Lion dance – Penang, 1981-1984.

Firecrackers to drive away evil Spirits from the home.

Thaipusam – is celebrated by Hindus to mark the victory of Lord Subramaniam over the demons, and is symbolic. Penang Festivals 1981-1984.

It is a day of penance, of thanksgiving for blessings received and the fulfillment of vows.

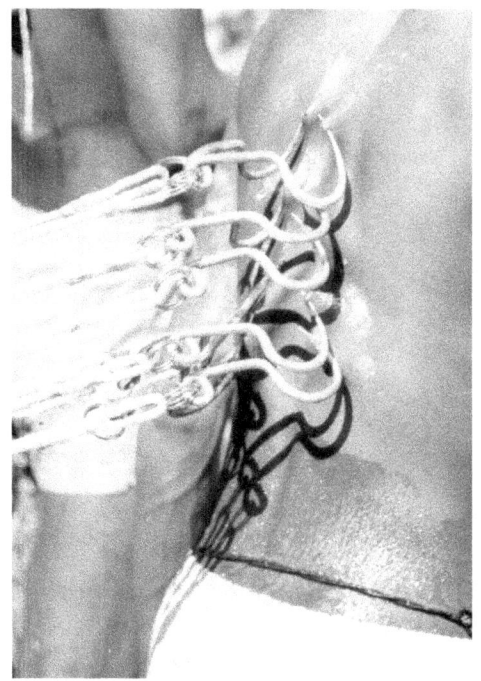

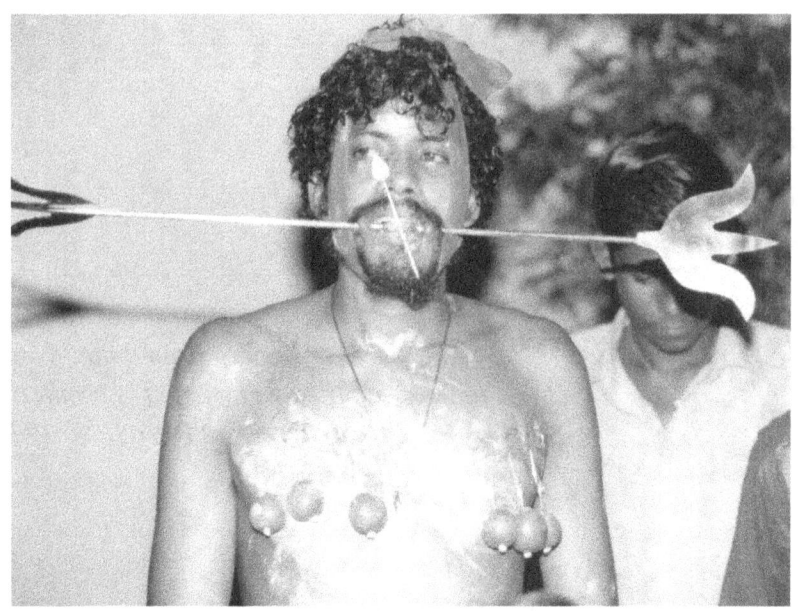

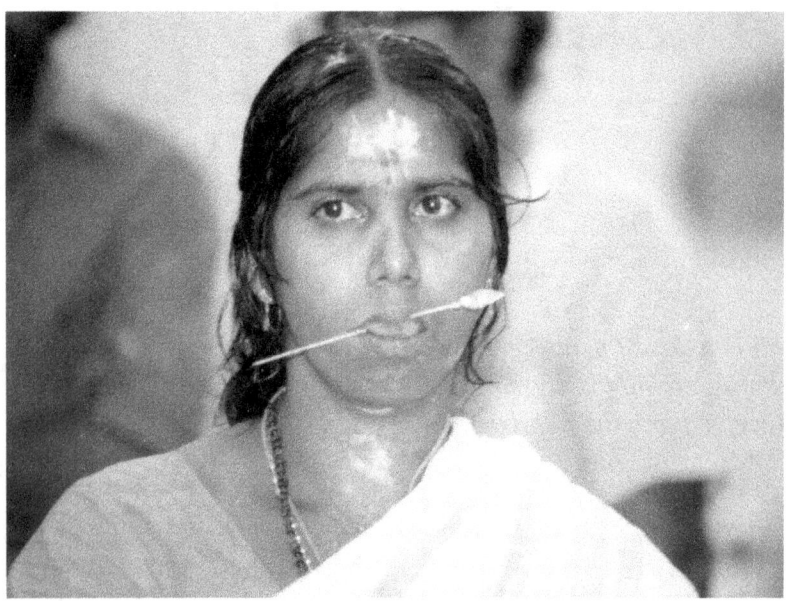

Thaipusam – Penang, Malaysia 1981-1984. A Devotee who has made a vow to the Lord carries out his/her commitment on this day. This may include piercing the body with different spears/hooks etc.

CHAPTER 38
CAR RALLY PENANG

I received my driving licence, in Brisbane, Queensland on the 30th August 1963 and from that date, until sometime in 1983, in Penang, Malaysia, I had never once been involved in a car rally. I did not have the faintest idea what a car rally involved and when I finished the car rally in Penang, I was still none the wiser.

I had been asked by another RAAF Police member, who I will call "Cinta" to be his navigator in a car rally which was being held on the island of Penang. This rally is held every year and sponsored by several big businesses on the Island. It was an event for the Malaysians however foreigners could enter as well. You could use any type of motor vehicle, Vintage, Veteran or whatever. Our vehicle was a Holden Kingswood which we hired on the Island to use as an unmarked Police Vehicle

From the very start we were in trouble, like a lot of other unsuspecting soles. The sponsor signs and numbers that we were to stick to the paintwork of our vehicles were not designed to come off, easily, as we found out later. We had to soak our signs off, inch by inch, using kerosene and rags. Months later, vehicles were still getting around Penang with half scraped off signs. Unfortunately a lot of people did not hear of kerosene and had used a scraper, which took off half the paintwork.

On entering the Car Rally we were given a sealed envelope which was supposed to contain directions along with a list of objects that we were supposed to collect along the way.

The envelope also contained the number of check points that we were required to register at, within a specified time. All well and good if you knew where you were bloody well going in the first place.

Another handy thing would have been if we were able to understand or read Malay, as some of the objects we collected were not what was required. When I agreed to navigate for Cinta, (I knew he would not let me drive), I thought, how hard could it be to read a map and after all, we were on an Island. We patrolled this Island and knew every track. How bloody wrong was I, we found bush tracks that we did not know existed; they had to be tracks because we run out of road and went bush. To make matters worse some stupid bugger would follow us and when we went bush, we could not turn the vehicle around and had to back out all the way that we had come.

To have someone else or another two to three vehicles behind you all having to back back, was ridiculous. It took hours. How did we get lost you asked? Well when I opened the envelope to look at the directions to follow for the rally, all I found were these little black lines on a paper with numbers at the end of the black lines. Some bloody map. I asked Cinta if he knew what we were supposed to do with this information and I could tell by his blank look, he didn't have a clue either. So as not to look completely stupid we decided to follow some of the other vehicles in front of us. One such fellow that I thought was completely useless to follow because he kept pushing his vehicle all over the Island, ended up winning the bloody trophy for the vehicle with the best fuel economy.

We managed the first three check points by following other vehicles, after that we ended up lost for the rest of the day. The first three check points were the only ones that really mattered anyway, according to Cinta. At the first check point we were given a Rally T-shirt, the next checkpoint a cap to go with our T-shirts and on the third check point a water bottle, empty of course. After that I don't think there were any more prizes, not that we would have known as we never saw another check point for the rest of the day. It was not until after we finished at the end of the day, was it explained to us that the black stick drawn on the paper was the direction that one travelled and the number at the end of the little black stick was the number of kilometers that you travelled before turning in the direction of your next little black stick. Stupid bloody map. We also decided not to enter any of the items that we collected during the rally as they would not have given us any point's only comical comments to be read out at the Rally Ball that night. How were we to know that a Drum Stick, in Malay, was a type of vegetable? We on the other hand drove into McTuckey or somewhere and saved two greasy chicken legs from our lunch. Our sea shells that we were supposed to collect from the sea shore, were collected somewhere inland, in the middle of the Island, and we had to buy the shells from some local kids. We were not the only ones to do this as some of the other idiots that followed us bought their sea shells from the same kids, but much cheaper. For these kids to have sea shells for sale, in the middle of Penang Island, must have known something about the idiots that go on these car rallies. After deciding that we had had enough of being lost for most of the day Cinta and I decided that we would head back to the Rally starting point to take the driving test as part of the competition. The competition consisted of the driver of the vehicle being able to complete a driving course while blind folded.

The navigator of the vehicle could walk beside the vehicle and guide the blind fold driver through the designated course. As Cinta and I had been driving around the Island, blind, for most of the day, we passed the course with flying colours. The rest of the afternoon was spent trying to remove the stupid bloody stickers from off of the vehicle without damaging the paint work. We attended the Rally Ball that night, which was terrific; we never received a Trophy of any kind or any mention of the two bloody stupid Australians. It would be another 11 years before another Car Rally was ever mentioned to me and I can assure you it was nothing like the Penang Car Rally.

CHAPTER 39

TOURS TO THAILAND – THIS SECTION IS DEDICATED TO MY MATE 'BLUE'

My wife and I had travelled to Thailand on many occasions while residing in Penang. We had visited many villages along the Thailand border, between Burma and Laos and had stayed overnight with some of the hill tribes. It was during one of these trips that after speaking with my regular Thai guide, I decided to organize a month long trip that was to take me off of the tourist track and visit the opium fields in the Golden Triangle.

As the trip would be too dangerous for my wife I decided to ask some of the RAAF Police members if they would be interested in such a trip. As I had previously worked in a Drug Investigation Section within the RAAF and had lectured RAAF members about the dangers of non-prescribed drugs I wanted to see the actual opium fields for myself. I also thought that if I was ever to work within a Drug Investigation Section again the experience of seeing the opium being cultivated would be of immense value. I was also interested in the fact that the photography of such an event would be an opportunity of a lifetime.

The trip took a year to plan and eventually three other RAAF Police members volunteered to accompany me on the trek. The four of us were to hire a pack bearer each and along with our guide we were a total of nine on the trip. The idea was to travel up or down the Mekong River by canoe, meet up with some elephant safari, then move away from the tourist track, on foot, staying with a different hill tribe each night. We had army rations and an extensive medical kit, all of which was carried by our pack bearers. In between our army rations we were to purchase fresh fruits etc as we went.

Before we commenced the trip we had checked with the local Thai Police and the American Embassy indicating where we might be heading and to see if there was any danger involved, as I did not want to put any member in harm's way. We were told by the American Embassy that there was a $2000 bounty on the head of any American caught out in the jungle, as America was trying to stop the drug trade in Thailand, Burma and Laos. As we would not be identified as Australians or treated any different from the Americans, our safety could not be guaranteed. We were offered weapons to carry during our trek.

I was not in favour of carrying any weapons as the locals looked all the same to me and I was there to shoot them with my camera not a rifle. The local Thai Police stated that once we left the tourist trail they also could not guarantee our safety. They could not guarantee your safety on the tourist trail not alone anywhere else.

The first two days of the trip went well as we traveled the Mekong River in canoes, arrived at our first village and collected our pack bearers. I had used the local Thai guide, Mr. Ead, on several of my trips to Thailand and I knew I could trust him, not to take any risks. At the end of the third day, having walked all day through the Thai hills, we stopped at a Mao hill tribe village where we would stay for the night. In the village we met two Frenchmen who had been touring the area just as we were. Unfortunately for the Frenchmen they had been attacked by some local bandits and stripped of everything that they owned.

All they were left with were their jocks. They had lost everything, passports, money, clothes, cameras etc. It was not good news. I advised Mr. Ead that I could not take the chance of having our group attacked and he told me not to worry as he would ensure that we had an armed escort for the remainder of the trip. I felt a lot happier with an armed escort as we came across other armed locals as well as the Burmese Army who had slipped across the border into Thailand for a rest between wars. More about the Burmese Army later.

After leaving the Mao village the next morning with our new armed escort, we had not travelled very far down the track, when we ran into a heavily armed group of villagers. Thank god they were not the Bandits as they were armed with M16 rifles and hand grenades. All these weapons against our guy carrying a lousy pistol. The villages were out looking for the Bandits that had attacked the two Frenchmen the day before. They were very friendly and invited us to stay the night in their village where they would entertain us with their dancing and music. Also they had some makeshift showers for us to use instead of washing in the freezing stream. That afternoon we took up their offer as we sat back and enjoyed a cold beer which they chilled for us in the local stream. No electricity in any of the villages that we encountered. The local beer was available in bottles throughout the Thai hills, along with bottles of coca cola. Cans of beer or anything in cans was not readily available to the hill tribes, so the sight of anything in a can was something out of the ordinary for them. We found this out when we discarded some small tins from our Army ration packs, as on doing so the locals would fight viciously over who was to own the can. To avoid further fights between villages we then had to give the village chief any of our empty cans so that he could distribute them evenly. In each village it was customary to set up our sleeping bags in the Village Chiefs hut. Normally there would be a large raised area of bamboo slats in the hut to lie on however at night the Chief , along with all his wives, would bring in all their animals, mainly pigs, and secure them under the bamboo slats. It was very hard to get to sleep with pigs and other animals running about underneath you at night. Another thing that would normally happen was that the wives would set about making a fire somewhere on the dirt floor of the hut, to cook meals.

For some reason they did not have a set fireplace. It was a bugger at night if you had to get out of bed and look for an outside toilet, as once you left your bamboo slats area; you had no idea where the hot coals of the fire might be so that you did not step on them. Another time I awoke very early one morning as my feet were hot. On looking down, the bottom of my sleeping bag and mosquito net were on fire. The Chiefs wives had made a new fire for the morning's breakfast at the bottom of my bed. It did not occur to them to wake me and tell me that my bed was on fire or to try and put it out. It was a bugger as I relied heavily on my mosquito net and now having a big hole one end, I could not keep out the mosquitoes.

We spent a lot of time visiting different hill tribe villages and the photography was just unbelievable. The people themselves were terrific and the countryside breathtaking. The locals wanted money if we wanted to take their photo, just a few baht (Thai money) however it would have been quite a nuisance for us to carry heavy coins around. The exchange rate at the time was ten Thai Baht, to one Malay Ringgit. Instead we purchased a large bag of lollies which we had to replace on a regular basis. Another item that we had to replace on a regular basis, which was much harder to replace, was our medical kit. We carried a rather large and expensive medical kit which we had put together over a period of time. It did not take long for the word to get around that we were a soft touch when it came to giving out medication and assisting in first aid. Each morning when we left a village there would be a string of people lined up along our next track hoping to be treated for their ills and wounds. We came across some very bad wounds like a spear through the foot and a machete cut through the top of a leg. We did not have much in the way of deadening pain, so removal of the spear took some time. The cut in the top of the leg with the machete was beyond anything we could do but recommend an immediate trip to a local doctor. Gangrene had already started in the leg wound. As it cost something like 1000 baht to visit a Doctor in Thailand it was unlikely that the patient would have taken our advice, as hill tribes rarely see

1000 baht. I was also quite shocked at the amount of villages suffering from some type of fever as well as TB. We were very careful where we ate and what we ate from, when visiting the villages. We carried all our own eating gear but you still had to be careful all the same.

Our four pack bearers would dose themselves up, each day, with some small white powder. When the drug kicked in they would take off and you would not see them for the rest of the day. When the drug wore off they were cot cases.

The local scenery was breathtaking, especially early morning with the mist rising off of the hills and streams. The rivers and streams were crystal clear and icy cold. It was easy to see how the locals could chill our beer in the nearby streams. It was hard to believe the humidity during the day and yet below freezing temperatures at night.

One morning, while making our way along a jungle path we came across a group of Soldiers from the Burmese Army. All were armed to the teeth; I had not seen the type of weapons that they were carrying, since my service in Vietnam.

The Soldiers had come across into Thailand for a rest as they were fighting some war in their country. At least I think they were in Thailand, we could have been in Burma for all I know as the border is not marked anywhere out there in the jungle. The Soldiers were fairly aggressive towards us at first and were eying off our Jungle Boots. They, on the other hand were wearing thongs. It was not until Mr. Ead spoke to them that they became friendlier. After we gave them some of our Army rations and shared some of our whisky with them, they allowed us to photograph them with all their weapons. They still wanted our GP (General Purpose) boots and even offered rifles and other military equipment for them.

Our GP boots were not for sale at any price as we needed them as much as they would have liked them. Oh yes, the whisky, purely medicinal purposes. The local whisky was bloody potent and if you did not like the taste you could always use it to light a fire, other than that it would also keep away the mosquitoes by rubbing it on your face and hands. I had never come across such an explosive cocktail

We walked countless miles, travelled on dusty tracks, wandered through deep jungle, passed thermal ponds and sometimes had the luxury of an overcrowded vehicle, winding around on dangerous roads. Eventually we got to witness the cultivation of the famous opium poppy. Unfortunately when we got to see the heroin factories they would not allow us to take photos. Another part of the trip that we never got to do was to go back onto the tourist trail and ride the elephants. It did not worry me that much as I had travelled that route, but it was a disappointment to one of the lads. However the experience and the photographs that we collected, we will probably never attain again.

During the last three days of the trip in the jungle, I was not feeling well, and by the time I reached Bangkok, the Capital of Thailand, I was running a terrible fever and had enormous lumps under my armpits. I went to a local doctor, however he did not seem to know what was wrong. When I arrived back at Butterworth I was rushed straight to the Base Hospital where I was diagnosed with blood poisoning. I had received some blisters from my boots while travelling in the hills of Thailand and replaced my footwear with thongs. I apparently picked up an infection through the burst blisters, possibly from buffalo urine on the track.

I spent a week in hospital, the Air Force was not impressed, but I had a fantastic time and I know the other lads enjoyed the trip as well.

I was to learn that one of the lads on the trip, a RAAF Policeman, passed away, suddenly, in 2006 at an early age. I dedicate this section of my book to you and your family, Blue, may you rest in peace, my friend.

MALAYSIA

It was hard to imagine that the Communists Insurgents were still active in some parts of Malaysia when we were there. It was not unusual to have little red flags placed around the Air Base by the Communists, just to let us know that they were still around. The placing of the flags would normally be at a date and time that was significant to them. We did not give a dam. I remember that any time that we travelled on duty, to areas of Malaysia, such as Ipoh, we had to have an armed escort as the Communists were still active along some areas of the highway. It was not until the 2nd December 1989 that the Communists Party officially surrendered and signed the Peace Accord with the Malaysian Government, in Haadyai, Thailand The Communist Party agreed to terminate hostility.

My wife and I will always have a place in our hearts for Malaysia, especially Penang. Go see Malaysia, especially Penang, there is a lot to see and do.

Go see Kek Lok Si Temple, the Temple of 1000 steps, or 1000 thieves, as some people called it. During the time my wife and I were there, all the local stall holders would sell their wares along the stairs of the Temple. We loved shopping there. Since the RAAF families have left Malaysia the stall holders are no longer at the Temple, as the Temple has been handed back to the Buddhists Monks .There is always the Snake Temple, the Reclining Buddha, or the Fort, to visit. The people are lovely and the food magnificent. It takes about 50 minutes to tour the Island. Tell them "Wheels" sent you. Err, second thoughts, better not, the Police are probably still looking for me, for something.

Trek to Thailand – Burma and Laos – On the train to Thailand, Author left, Garry centre and Roy standing.
Below – Arrival Thailand, Blue left, Author at rear, Roy right and Thai guide, Mr. Ead centre.

Thailand Trek – Travelling the Mekong River on our way to our first village. We collected our four backpack bearers before travelling up river. All up there were nine of us on the trip.
Below – A rest stop on way to our second village, we travelled several kilometers on foot, that day.

Thailand Trek – Some of the local scenery in Thailand as we walked along the dusty tracks.

Thailand Trek – Local hill tribes that we encountered in one of the many villages that we visited during the trip.

The little lass is unhappy as she just had some haemorrhoids cut out of her back passage, with a pen knife, by her dad and doused with lighter fluid to stop infection.

Thailand Trek – Local hill tribes encountered on the trip. The boys, below, were not that keen on washing, I do not blame them as the water was freezing.

Thailand Trek – Each night the occupants of a village would put on their best clothes and sing and dance for us, they were such lovely people and made us very welcome. Below – Garry and Blue looking for a shallow area to cross a stream.

Thailand Trek – Blue, Garry and Mr. Ead inspecting raw opium, which most of the hill tribes seem to smoke on a daily basis. Below – Opium smoker, this chap had difficulty even to sit up as the opium made him very tired.

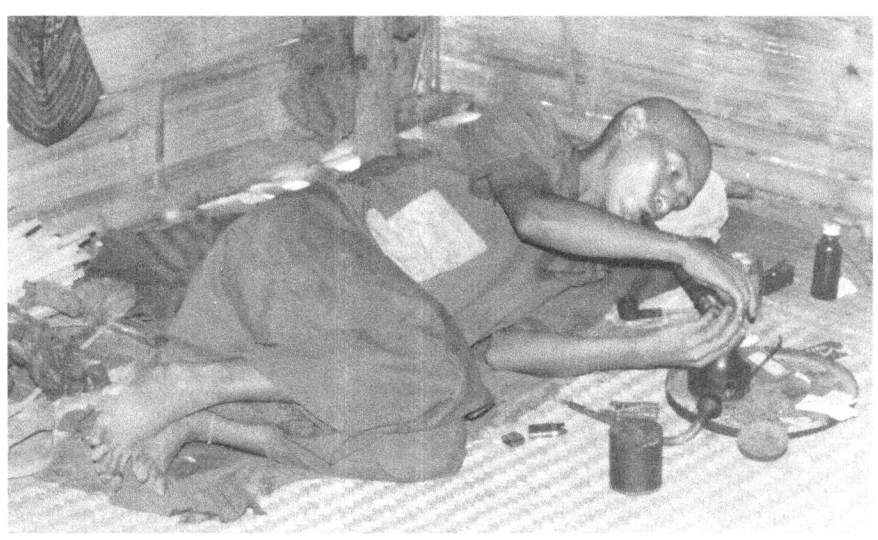

Thailand Trek – The Author and Roy sorting out Army rations for evening meal. Left – Blue taking a short break as we make our way along the dusty track.

Thailand Trek – Soldier from Burma, not sure who he was fighting, I suspect he was fighting the official Burmese Army. Below – Blue checking out the weight of the Machine Gun rounds carried by the soldiers.

Thailand Trek – Poppy/Opium field. We were being shown how the raw opium is collected. Below – the collection of the raw opium, up close.

Thailand Trek – Garry and Roy checking out a manual grain crusher in one of the villages.
Below – Garry and Roy asking for the Medical kit to attend to the local male who had shot himself in the foot with an arrow.

Thailand Trek – Heroin Factories along the Mekong, Burma and Laos.

Thailand Trek – Almost at the end of our Trek, note the thongs, as most of us had blisters on our feet. The Author, second in from right, contacted blood poisoning from burst blisters on feet.
Below – Thailand Tourist Police.

CHAPTER 40
LEAVING MALAYSIA

Penang, Malaysia 1981-1984 – Penang Ferries in the foreground. The Komtar, (high rise, round building) still being built. This building caught fire on the top, three floors, while still being built.

In December 1984, my wife and I left Malaysia as I had been poster to RAAF Base Pearce, in Western Australia. I had some concerns about the posting as I had never applied to be posted to the West at any time. I had requested a posting to Queensland as I was thinking of leaving the RAAF within the next eighteen months, to look for civil employment. I received a good assessment report each year while serving the three years in Malaysia.

On making enquiries with the RAAF as to the possibility of being promoted while being posted to RAAF Pearce, I was informed that there was no vacancy for a Flight Sergeant in Western Australia. It looked like I had killed the china man again. I advised the RAAF that I believed that I might be due to be promoted within the next six months. The information that I received back was that if I were to be promoted, then I would most likely be posted to the eastern states. When I asked about my furniture coming from Malaysia and the furniture that I had in storage, in Adelaide, I was informed that the Air Force would pay to have it delivered to any eastern states posting. As I only had eighteen months left to serve however I would have to sign on to have my furniture shifted again at RAAF expense. I was not pleased as it seemed like some form of blackmail.

My wife and I liked Perth so much that we decided to purchase a home in suburban Edgewater. Our furniture from Malaysia and our furniture from Adelaide arrived one day apart. The 44 crates of furniture and personal items that had been so well packed in Malaysia, had now been unpacked by who I don't know, prior to being delivered at our premises. The damage that had now been caused to our furniture and some missing items left a bitter taste. It was impossible to move all the furniture and personal items from where they had been delivered to our driveway, into the safety of our premises, all in one day. I had to spend the night checking the furniture, out in the driveway, in case someone decided to walk off with it. I had put 15 years of my life into the RAAF and this was not how we were supposed to be treated.

Above – Penang Bridge, joining mainland, Butterworth to Penang Island – 2005. Construction of this bridge had not commenced when Author left Penang in 1984. Below – Penang city 2005.

Above – The old Raffles Hotel, Singapore, restored to its former glory, as seen in 2005. Left – Kek Lok Si Temple, Penang as seen again in 2005. Temple of a 1000 steps. Local markets no longer operate from Temple, handed back to Monastery.

CHAPTER 41
RAAF BASE – PEARCE – WESTERN AUSTRALIA

RAAF Base Pearce 1985 – The Author and wife Joy at a RAAF Sergeants Mess, Dining In night, prior to the Author being promoted to Flight Sergeant.

I had to report for duties at RAAF Pearce within a couple of days after my arrival in Perth. I was determined, whether I was to be promoted or not, to see out the next eighteen months doing the job that I loved and to the best of my ability. I was employed at Pearce as a RAAF Police Patrol, Shift Supervisor and later reassigned to Special Investigations as the Senior NCO in charge.

The Air Base at Pearce was again, an operational base; therefore the work load in any position involving the RAAF Police was demanding. The base is patrolled by Police Dogs which help protect the Aircraft and RAAF installations. There was not only the base to patrol but RAAF Pearce has large areas of land outside of the base, including a married quarters area, large bombing range, Telecommunications Unit and other areas, all of which are out of bounds to the general public. These areas have to be secured and checked on a regular basis. The Great Northern Highway which runs past the Air Base sees its fair share of civilian Traffic Accidents and at times the closest emergency vehicles are those of the RAAF Police.

While stationed at Pearce I was attached to RAAF Support Unit, Canberra to attend Number 2/85 Australian Federal Police Traffic Accident Investigators Course. I did not advise the instructors of my driving skills or my firsthand knowledge of Traffic Accidents while serving with the RAAF in Malaysia.

No sooner had I arrived back at Pearce from the Traffic Accident Course, I was sent on an exchange assignment to the Western Australian Police, Fingerprint Section. I enjoyed working in the Fingerprint Section as I got to travel all over Perth and lift prints from several crime scenes. On returning to Pearce after my stint with the WA Police, I was to learn that the Sergeant I was working with in the Criminal Investigation section had been posted. The Sergeant was replaced by a Senior Corporal. It was not long before the Corporal was sent on a WA Detective Training Course and I was left alone to handle any Investigations on the base.

During the first 6 months at RAAF Pearce, I served under a RAAF Provost Officer who wanted the RAAF Police to be involved in as many police courses as possible, hence all the training courses. I did not mind as I thought that you could never have enough training.

This Officer also sent me along to the Rifle Range on the Base to instruct the Reservists on the use of the SLR (Self Loading Rifle) which was the basic weapon in use at the time for most of the services. I had to draw the line however when he wanted to send me bush on training exercises. I was working in my office when the Officer came in and said 'Sergeant, how would you like to go out on a training exercise for a few days, it will mean jungle greens, backpack, army rations, sleeping in tents etc?' My reply, 'Unless you make it an order Sir, not bloody likely.' 'I have seen enough of the bush, jungle greens, bloody rations and tents, to last me a bloody lifetime.' I said. 'After six years in the Army and three bloody wars, who in their right mind would volunteer for that?' I said.

'I am going.' said the Officer. 'I wish you all the best Sir' With that he left me mumbling something about ex-grunts.

Having read the first part of this book, you will remember that it was at RAAF Base Pearce that the RAAF Police worked with the Special Air Services Regiment (SASR). The Regiment was using several of the buildings on the base for training purposes. One large hangar on the base was being used to interrogate prisoners. The prisoners were their own SASR troops who were undergoing training in case they were ever taken prisoner. These guys trained for real as the prisoners were subject to harsh treatment, liked being stripped naked in the middle of winter and hosed down with a fire hose until they surrendered something. I could not believe that one of the prisoners, a Sergeant, had actually volunteered to undergo the course for a second time. I said all along they were mad, but seeing them in action and having worked occasionally with the SASR in Vietnam, they certainly are our finest. One of the other buildings on the Base, which was a Living in Airmen's Quarters, was vacant and undergoing an upgrade, new paint, carpets etc. The OC of the base, being no doubt most generous, allowed the SASR to use this building for training while it remained vacant. I do not think the OC realized what type of training the SASR wanted to do in the building as when they kicked doors of hinges, blew out windows etc, I think he was horrified. One of our Airmen, who had had a few to many drinks, wandered into the building on his way home from the boozer and received a broken nose, for being in the wrong place at the wrong time. These guys play rough. I believe after the damage to the building was realized, the SASR were not permitted to blow up anything else on the base. It was a good time and I enjoyed working with the SASR once again.

It was six months to the day of my arriving at RAAF Base Pearce when I was told to front up and see the CO, Base Squadron. As I made my way towards the Office I kept thinking to myself, what the bloody hell have I done now, I can't think of anyone that I have upset lately, I don't know, I will just have to wait and see. My fears were soon laid to rest, as on fronting the Commanding Officer he walked around from behind his desk and shook my hand, congratulating me on my promotion to Flight Sergeant. It was a lovely feeling, one which I will remember for a long time. I did not have a lot to do with the CO Base Squadron as I did not deal with him directly in my Police work as we had a Provost Officer on the base, in charge of the RAAF Police. The Commanding Officer still knew a lot about me and complemented me on my work since I had been at Pearce. I was a little surprised but the fact that we had a terrific Provost Officer in charge of our section, made all the difference. Along with the promotion came a date for a posting to RAAF Base Williamtown, NSW. I was to be at my new posting before Christmas and I was snowed under with investigations and still working by myself. It would be another three to four months until my position at RAAF Pearce could be filled. As the only other Investigator was on a Detective Training course it meant that the base would be left without an Investigator, once I left on posting. A request for an extension of time was granted for me to remain at Pearce for another two to three months until the Base could arrange for my replacement.

I could not believe what happened next as I was to remain at RAAF Pearce until the 26th February 1986. My first major investigation was to carry out a Security Survey of the Base Telecommunications Unit.

I am not going to bore you with a list of requirements for such a task only to tell you it is a daunting task for two or more investigators not alone one. It took me two months to complete the Survey. First my Security clearance had to be upgraded before I commenced the task. This clearance only lasted until the job was completed. Every fence, wall, window, roof, door has to be checked before you even start on the personnel. Original plans of the building, if available, are required so that you can check items like fire ratings for doors, sprinkler systems, fire hoses etc. The work is time consuming. After hours checks of the building would be required, then you would have to look at what security measures are in place and are they being carried out correctly. You are required to look for security weaknesses involving the Building along with any Security problems involving Personnel. Should you require expert help on any particular problem then this would have to be arranged. Once you had completed the survey, it would then have to be typed up into a suitable report detailing any problems that you found along with suitable recommendations to fix the problems. Photographs would also accompany the report. I did not need this type of investigation when I was trying to clear my desk prior to my posting to Williamtown.

It was a few days before Christmas 1985 and I was still involved with the Security Survey, when I received a telephone call from the base Sergeants Mess Secretary to say that there had been a robbery and that I needed to attend the mess immediately. To cut a long story short the safe in the Sergeants mess along with the Mess Fees Box, in the same room, had been emptied sometime during the time that the Mess was open to Christmas drinks between the base Officers Mess/Sergeants Mess. What made the whole investigation difficult was that the robbery had been made easy because some clown left the keys to the safe, in the safe lock and the room containing the safe, open. I was looking at somewhere between 60-80 people to interview. Some of these people had already left the base on Christmas leave.

Obviously someone had a great spend up over Christmas as the safe contained several thousand dollars. I asked the civil Police to attend however once they found out that the keys had been left in the safe and the room containing the safe, left open; they were not interested in investigating the matter and wished me luck. I also believe at the time the Provost Officer on the base had requested assistance from the local RAAF Police Detachment. I cannot remember as to why the Detachment did not attend at the time. I spent all Christmas and New Year carrying out interviews of all known RAAF members that were in the Sergeants Mess on the night of the robbery. Unfortunately after taking statements from over 60 plus members, no one had seen or heard anything involving the robbery. Any fingerprints found on the safe were useless unless we could come up with a possible suspect. I was not in a position to fingerprint 60 plus members. Much to my disappointment the offender/s responsible for the robbery were never caught. All I could do was make recommendations so that the access to the safe and the room containing the safe, were never again made easy access to a would be thief.

Also the person responsible for leaving the keys in the safe, I would have recommended disciplinary action. I would have also recommended disciplinary action against the person responsible for leaving the door open to the room containing the safe.

It was now January 1986, I was still carrying out interviews involving members who had been present in the Sergeants Mess during the night the Safe and Mess Fees Box were robbed. These members were not available over Christmas and were now returning to the base from Christmas leave. I needed to finalize the Investigation so that I could complete my Investigation Report prior to my posting to Williamtown.

I needed another Investigation, prior to my posting, like a hole in the head. I was to investigate the death of a RAAF member who had committed suicide by gassing himself in his motor vehicle. I do not intend to go into any detail in fairness to the member and his family. Suicides of any kind are not nice to investigate and if people could see how they die, when taking their own life, I feel sure that they would think twice before they would carry out such an act. Looking back on my career in the RAAF I estimate that I would have investigated at least one suicide every 18-24 months. People reading this book would find that hard to believe. But think about it, I served on eight RAAF Units during my time as a RAAF Policeman and carried out numerous investigations at other RAAF Units. A total of 16 years. That is a hell of a lot of people taking their own life. I do not think however these figures would only involve the RAAF, my guess is the Army and the Navy would have similar figures. I could be wrong but I know the figures that I was involved in during my time as a RAAF Policeman, I have no reason to lie and every suicide is recorded. The figures therefore would be in the archives.

RAAF Base Pearce 1985 – The Author carrying out part of a Security Survey, to see if the key pad security system can be bypassed.

RAAF Base Pearce, Western Australia. The Author, examining a blood trail left at the scene of wilful damage caused to the glass panel door, leading to the Airmen's Canteen. The blood trail lead to the base Medical Centre where the offender had been admitted due to his injuries. The offender was identified and charged with wilful damage.

CHAPTER 42

RAAF BASE – WILLIAMTOWN

RAAF Police Section, RAAF Base Williamtown. NSW 1986. Author front row, first on left. Final posting, prior to Discharge from the RAAF.

I managed somehow to clear my desk at RAAF Base Pearce prior to my posting to RAAF Base Williamtown. I arrived at my new posting on the 26th February 1986 and took up the position as the Flight Sergeant in charge of the RAAF Police Investigation Section, BSWLM (Base Squadron Williamtown). I arrived at the base unaccompanied as I decided to live in on the base for the next 12 months, so that my wife could remain in our home in Western Australia. I had a Sergeant RAAF Policeman with me in the Investigation section who I had worked with at RAAF Base Laverton, Victoria. We were both Corporals at the time and I knew him as "The Bacardi Kid" The "Kid" and I got on well and we were responsible for all criminal investigations on the base.

Williamtown was an operational base, it was the new home of the RAAF F18 Aircraft, referred to as "The Hornet" There was plenty of work on the Base for two investigators as we were to discover. As I was on call 24 hours a day while living in on the base I managed to build up plenty of overtime. I used the extra time to fly back to Perth occasionally, to spend time with my wife. The time went quickly. Once again while working on the base I was fortunate enough to work with the RAAF Police Dog Section. I had worked with some of the members while serving with the RAAF in Malaysia.

The RAAF had a fitness standard which had to be passed once a year, unfortunately so did the RAAF Police. Like all other RAAF Police I had to pass both fitness tests each year. To do this I had to keep fit, which for me, meant I had to jog around the Base Airfield at least once a day, either before breakfast or late in the afternoon. I had always had trouble with pain in the base of my spine since a Parachuting accident during my time with the Army, in Malaysia in 1965. I was not aware that jogging around the Base on bitumen was to aggravate the damage to the base of my spine, so much so that my last month on the base was spent in hospital with my legs in traction. More about that later.

During the year I spent at RAAF Williamtown the Military Law was to change where the RAAF Police not only had the power of arrest for all Services, Army, Navy as well as the RAAF, but the Tri-Service Law came in as well. This involved two important changes regarding the way we carried out Police interviews and powers of search. The new Tri-Service law meant that the Airman/Woman who was being interviewed as a suspect for an offence could ask for a lawyer being present. The lawyer could be a RAAF Lawyer or the serviceman/woman could opt to hire a private lawyer. This was something we did not have to face under the old military law. The other change was the power of search. Under the old type Military Law we could search a suspect's room or married quarter with or without his/her permission. Under the new Tri-Service law we needed a search warrant, which was not that easy to obtain. What this also meant was that petty theft, like a stolen Tarmac Jacket, was no longer that easy to investigate. I could not see anyone issuing a search warrant to search a suspect's room for a Tarmac Jacket. It made our work in the RAAF rather difficult as we had not been trained to deal with civilian Lawyers. I do not know what system is in place in the Service now, all I know is that the new laws made my job very difficult.

The last major investigation that I was involved in while serving at RAAF Williamtown involved a Court Marshall. Three Airmen had been charged with the death of a cat and her kittens. I will not go into details only to say the animals died a horrible death, the case was proven and two of the Airmen deserved a lot more punishment than they received. The investigation into the deaths of the animals was quite involved, unfortunately The Truth newspaper had been made aware of the offence committed on the base before my offsider and I had time to complete the investigation. This no doubt placed a lot of pressure on both of us as I know that the time I spent in the Base Hospital with the damage to my spine, I suffered from a stress related illness as well. A combination between not knowing if I would walk again and my previous work load, took its toll on me mentally. It was not long after leaving the Service that I was diagnosed with severe Post Traumatic Stress Disorder

On requesting my discharge from the RAAF after 16 years as a RAAF Policeman, I was sent back to RAAF Base Pearce in Western Australia, in December 1986, to complete my final two weeks in the RAAF and to arrange my transformation from Service life to Civilian life.

With my previous six years Army Service and now 16 years with the RAAF, I had now completed 22 years Military Service. I limped away from the RAAF on the 18th December 1986. I could not straighten up due to the damage to my spine and it would take another 12 months before I could once again walk, upright and seek gainful employment. I would persevere for another 13 years in the workforce with the damage to my spine and medication for my PTSD, until finally I needed crutches to walk any distance and the medication for my PTSD had doubled in the dosage required. The medication for the pain in my spine is a Morphine base medication and the medication for my PTSD is so strong that I cannot drive when using it. In the meantime I lost all the hearing in my left ear and on a permanent basis.

RAAF Base, Williamtown, NSW 1986 – RAAF Police Dog Handler – K.Lilly. Kim worked with the Author at Williamtown, is a close friend, and was responsible for the cartoons in the Authors first book,

GREEN MULES GREEN GIANTS.

CHAPTER 43
CONCLUSION

I grew up in a loving family, the youngest of nine children. My parents had both passed away by the time I was 15 years old. I was raised by my sisters and brothers. One of my brothers, Lionel (Tiny), served in the Australian Army as a Sapper. He was part of the Commonwealth Forces and served in the Occupation of Japan after WWII. Two of my sisters, June/Rhonda served in the Australian Army as WRAAC's. I grew up around Military uniforms; therefore it was understandable that I would one day wear a Military uniform of my Country. I did not plan on wearing two types of uniforms and serving 22 years in the service. I also did not plan on serving overseas on active service, however I was well aware that by putting on a Military uniform, that I might one day be required to lay down my life for my country. I have lost count of the times that I have walked away and survived different events and can only assume that my time to depart this earth has not arrived.

My biggest problem when joining the RAAF was that I had already served six years in the Australian Army as an Infantry Soldier. I spent almost three, out of the six years, on active service. Had I not served in the Army prior to my enlistment into the RAAF, I may have had a totally different view of service life. I was fortunate when joining the RAAF in 1971, I was not sent overseas again for another ten years. Life in the RAAF was quite tame compared to what I had been through in the Army. The RAAF in some way gave me a chance, not only to get my life back in some sort of order, (for a while anyway) but gave me the opportunity to gain a better education, to which I am grateful.

The RAAF also gave me the chance to work with some great people, people from all walks of life, but once within the service, all dedicated to the work at hand. Each person bringing with them a wealth of knowledge and experience. The Service was always a learning curve and the RAAF Police mustering no different. I learnt from some of the best.

There is no doubt that I probably upset a few RAAF members during my RAAF career, even within my own mustering. I think that this is unavoidable when there is any type of Rank structure involved. Prior to my Discharge from the RAAF I was offered a Commission in Administration and told that I could remuster to a Provost Officer at a later date. We all know about the promise of remusters, don't we? I was also informed that if I accepted a Commission it would add a compulsory two years to my service. I had to step back and consider my future. I was 41 years of age, not in the best of health and sick of moving my family from State to State. The decision therefore, to walk away from the Service after 22 years, was not that hard to make.

I regret none of the 22 years that I spent in the Services, especially the 16 years that I served as a RAAF Policeman. Would I do it all again? "Where is my Uniform?"

I feel however that now, my 68 year old body would have other ideas as I need crutches to walk any distance, medication for the pain in my spine, medication for my PTSD and two hearing aids which are completely bloody useless. The passion is there but little else.

My three children saw me wear two types of Military uniform, the Baggy Greens and the Blue Suit. They too have served in uniform, my daughter, a short time as a Police Cadet in the Northern Territory, before an injury ruined her career. She was then redeployed into Community Policing for two years. My daughter also serving sometime in the Australian Navy Reserve. My two boys also served in the Royal Australian Navy, my youngest in the Reserves, my oldest boy serving 10 years and reaching the rank of Naval Lieutenant. I think the Easterby family have more than done their share for this wonderful country we call Australia. No regrets and no complaints from any one of us.

I was fortunate to have been part of a wonderful organization of dedicated Military personnel in the Royal Australian Regiment, the RAAF Police and Police Dog Mustering.

No doubt there will be the armchair critics, who after having read this book, will say that this is not right, or that is wrong. All I can say is that I am not into research; I relied on my memory after 47 years, working from bunker to bunker and Base to Base. After all this time I am now a Senior and entitled to my Senior moments. I have left behind a record of events for my children; you could have done the same.

Once again thank you to all those members involved in the Royal Australian Regiment, the RAAF Police Mustering, past and present.

If you enjoyed my book tell a friend, if not tell them "Wheels" wrote it and they will have to read it to find out who the bloody hell is "Wheels".

Tony Wayne Easterby
Ex – Corporal Infantry Soldier – 2RAR – 4RAR
Ex- Flight Sergeant/RAAF Police

ABOUT THE AUTHOR

Tony Wayne Maurice Easterby, born 30th August 1946, Brisbane, Queensland, Australia. Youngest of nine children, five Sisters, three Brothers. Raised by Sisters/Brothers, having lost both parents by the age of 15. Growing up with a Brother and two Sisters serving in the Australian Army it seemed only natural that the youngest sibling would follow in their footsteps.

Joining the Australian Army at 18 years of age the Author saw active service in Malaysia, Borneo and Vietnam by the age of 22. Wounded in Vietnam in 1968, the Author left the Army a few months later to work the then Father-in-laws farm, Balaklava, South Australia. After an unsuccessful two years of farm life the Author decided to re-enlist in the Services, this time as a Policeman with the Royal Australian Air Force. Serving 16 years with the RAAF, combined with Army Service, a total of 22 years Military Service was achieved.

GLOSSARY OF TERMS AND ABBREVIATIONS

ANZAC	Australian and New Zealand Army Corps
APC	Armoured Personnel Carrier M113 Track Vehicle
ARVN	Army of the Republic of Vietnam
Bait	Term used by writer to describe food poisoning
Bandoleers	Shoulder belts made by joining M60 Machine Gun belts together
Batman	No relation to Robin, Soldier acting as Aid to Officer, Servant
Brew Up	To boil the Billy, to make tea or coffee
Canungra JTC	Canungra Jungle Training Centre. Approximately 20klm inland from Gold Coast, QLD
Charlie	Nickname for Viet Cong or VC Victor Charlie
Chopper	Helicopter
Clacker	A firing device which generates its own power to detonate a Claymore Anti-Personnel Mine
Claymore (mine)	A curve shaped Anti-Personnel Mine which can be fired singly or in groups. M18-A1

Click	One Mile, now One Kilometer
Communist Insurgents	Malay/Chinese Guerrilla Forces, Terrorists
Company	Consists of 3 Platoons, Support Group and One Officer, approximately 120 plus men
Corporal	NCO, Non Commission Officer, Rank within service
CSM	Company Sergeant Major (W02, Warrant Officer Class 2
Dyaks	Natives of Borneo, two types, Sea Dyaks and Land Dyaks
Detonator	Item to help set of explosion
Dhobi Rash	Dhobi – Indian Laundryman. Clothes belonging to several people would be washed together in same dirty water. Resulted in skin problems under arms and crotch areas
Dog Tags	Nickname for two stainless steel name tags carried by all soldiers around neck, tags contain full name, service number, date of birth and blood group of wearer
F111	Supersonic Long Range Strike Aircraft
Gun Group	Two soldiers who operate the Section Machine Gun (M60). Number One operates the gun while Number Two helps feed in belt rounds and with barrel changes etc.
Gunner	Term used by writer to describe Number One operator of Machine Gun

Gurkhas	Nepalese Soldier serving in British or Indian Army
Hand Grenade	M26 described under weapons
Harbour Position	A tactical, static position taken up day or night by soldiers in the field Usually by Platoons/Companies Standard formation procedure.
Hoochie/Hutchie	Nickname for personal tent or lodgings
Lance Corporal	First rank up from Private Soldier – Leading Aircraftsman equivalent rank in RAAF
Landmine	Mine laid in ground, Anti-Personnel or Vehicle type
Long Johns	Term used by writer to describe winter underwear
LSD	Lyserigic Acid Diethylamide (Hallucinogens Drug)
Metho	Methylated Spirits
Mike Squad	ARVN Ranger Unit
NAAFI Store	Navy, Army, Air Force, Institute. British Duty Free Store
National Serviceman	Conscript Soldier, 2 year Army Service
Nui Dat	Main Base in Vietnam for Australian Task Force and Support Units
NVA	North Vietnamese Army

Officer	Commissioned Rank
Orang-Utan	Large Anthropoid Ape
Password	Selected word or phrase known only to one's own side and used to distinguish friend or foe (enemy)
Picket	Used in this text as small body of men on Military Duty
Platoon	Normally consists of three sections of 10 men, Officer, Batman and Signal Operator, approximately 33 men
Poppy	Papaver Somniferum – annual herb, native South-eastern Europe, Western Asia- also known as the Opium Poppy
PX	American Duty Free Store
RAAF	Royal Australian Air Force
RAF	Royal Air Force (British)
RAR	Royal Australian Regiment
Rifleman	Basic Infantry Soldier, issued with standard SLR Rifle during writer's service
1RTB	1 Recruit Training Battalion (Kapooka) Wagga Wagga, NSW
SASR	Special Air Service Regiment
Signalman	Radio Operator

Spit Polish	Saliva from mouth mixed with shoe Polish to help shine boots/shoes
Tail End Charlie	Nickname used for last Rifleman travelling behind group of soldiers
Tiger Suit	Camouflage Uniform normally worn In Vietnam by ARVN Rangers
Toggle Rope	Standard issue nylon rope with loop at both ends
Trooper	Term used by writer to describe his own and other section members
Viet Cong	Main Fighting Force of National Liberation Front, North Vietnam
VC	Viet Cong or 'Victor Charlie'
Wait-a-While	Nickname given to vine containing small sharp thorns which act like the teeth of a saw if not treated with care
WRAAF (pronounced WAF)	Women's Royal Australian Air Force
Yanks	Nickname for Americans

WEAPONS – GLOSSARY OF TERMS AND ABBREVIATIONS

Bren Gun	Light Machine Gun (WW2) US 30 round magazine, weapon converted to fire 7.62mm during writers Service.
BGPMG	British General Purpose Machine Gun –7.62mm belt fed.
Browning	.50" calibre M2 Machine Gun – belt fed Automatic
GPMG (M60)	General Purpose Machine Gun -7.62mm belt fed
HE	High Explosive
MG	Machine Gun
M16	Armalite Rifle 5.56mm US
M26	Grenade Fragmentation US –high explosive
M60	General Purpose Machine Gun – 7.62mm belt fed
M79	Grenade Launcher – Single Barrel 40mm
mm	Calibre
PE	Plastic Explosive
RPG	Rocket Propelled Grenade-B40 or RPG2
SLR	Self Loading Rifle,7.62mm, gas and spring operated. Issue to Australian Infantry Soldier during writer's service and Vietnam war.

www.ingramcontent.com/pod-product-compliance
Lightning Source LLC
Chambersburg PA
CBHW071225080526
44587CB00013BA/1497